THE LITTLE BOOK OF TOOLS

HOW TO CHANGE THE PATTERNS WE PRACTICE

JESSICA NEIDEFFER

BALBOA
PRESS

A DIVISION OF HAY HOUSE

Balboa Press books may be ordered through booksellers or by contacting:

Balboa Press
A Division of Hay House
1663 Liberty Drive
Bloomington, IN 47403
www.balboapress.com
1 (877) 407-4847

Print information available on the last page.

ISBN: 978-1-9822-1901-7 (sc)
ISBN: 978-1-9822-1900-0 (hc)
ISBN: 978-1-9822-1909-3 (e)

Library of Congress Control Number: 2018915053

Balboa Press rev. date: 04/03/2019

CONTENTS

Dedication vii

Preface ix

Introduction xvii

Tool #1:   Creating Safe Space in the Mind 1

Tool #2:   Shift Your Language and Perspective 7

Tool #3:   Ritual & Meditation 15

Tool #4:   The Cutting of the Cords................................... 21

Tool #5:   The Practice of BEing… Non-Attached 29

Tool #6:   Let Go of Unloving Feelings 35

Tool #7:   Awareness of the Roles We Choose 41

Tool #8:   Let Go of Labels and Expectations 47

Tool #9:   Awareness & Eradication of Self-Importance...... 55

Tool #10: Mirror Work.. 63

Tool #11: Write Your Way to Freedom 69

Tool #12: Reintegrate Other Versions of the Self 75

Tool #13: Healing with Sound... 81

Tool #14: BEing Grounded When Creating......................... 87

Tool #15: Cultivating Relationships and Abundance 93

Tool #16: Manifest Your Dreams & Desires 101

The Beginning 107

Answers to The Money Exercise in TOOL #15 111

References...113

DEDICATION

This book is dedicated to ALL Inhabitants of the Earth and Beyond... without one of you, the entire experience is completely different. Thank You for BEing here!

And special thanks to Julie Larson for her friendship, perspective, and editing skills.

PREFACE

The conscious part of my journey began in 2007 after experiencing extreme symptoms of vertigo. I went to a chiropractor for help and my symptoms went away within a few weeks. After a few adjustments, he suggested that massage would support me in continuing my healing process. I made an appointment with the therapist he recommended and at the end of the massage she offered 15 minutes of Reiki for free. I said, "What's that?". She shared with me that she was going to place her hands on the different chakras (energy centers) of my body to help me move "negative" energies out and restore balance. I asked what I was supposed to do, and she told me that I would just lay there and rest a little longer. I agreed and then proceeded to leave my body when she placed her hands on my chest, or what is called the "heart chakra" in Vedic Healing. I had experienced unseen energies or what people might call spirits at a very early age but did not understand or know how to communicate with them. However, I had never experienced being outside of my body before, so you can imagine how surprising this was at first.

I was fully conscious, floating above my body at the ceiling of the massage room. I feel like the shock of the moment actually allowed me to observe myself instead of reacting and falling out of it. As I observed the therapist with her hands on my chest from above, I watched the picture of us below change to a black and white X-ray and then I was able to see my rib cage and my heart inside. I also noticed a lock on my ribs over my heart. The lock was like the small combination locks I have used for my bike in the past. As I became aware of it, I saw it shatter into a million pieces and watched my rib cage open like two barn doors. Once the doors opened, my heart flew out of my chest and I returned to my body on the massage table, now watching a TV screen in my mind's eye. My heart, now floating above me, looked like a cartoon heart… bright red, with a big, cheesy smile and angel wings. As it smiled at me, I heard a man's voice say, "You are free!". The voice was even more shocking to me because it was just the female massage therapist and I in the room.

When I heard these words, I asked, "What does that mean?" and was shown in my mind all the times from age 5 to that present moment when I was in pain or feeling ill. In each of the instances I saw myself putting my hands on the areas experiencing pain and asking God or Jesus to take that pain away. I kept thinking, "I wish that was real!" and then the voice came through again assuring me that it was and that I was this healing energy. I understood then that I was supposed to start practicing Reiki to learn (remember) how to heal myself and others on a deeper, emotional, even cellular level. In that moment, I had no idea what any of that looked like, but I knew I had to start bringing this practice into my life and share it with others. The voice continues to come to me at pivotal moments in my life to guide me when the direction changes. It shares with me how to move forward and I have come to know that it is my true voice and I do my best to follow it every time.

After this initial opening and new awareness, I consciously started setting intentions to invite teachers into my life. As the old saying goes, "When the student is ready, the teacher will appear". Actually, many teachers appeared and one in particular had a major influence in my awakening, but he did not show up until four years later. I was so excited to immerse myself in this new experience and all the possibilities that came along with it! The excitement that I felt as I received and shared new information just seemed to attract everything and everyone that I was seeking. I would have a conversation with one person and that would lead to them introducing me to someone else with a new and different concept. As I gathered more information, more opportunities to learn and expand arrived. There always seemed to be an event offering a new experience like Reiki shares, as well as traditional Native American sweat lodge and drum circles. I did my best to attend everything that I was able to and read as much as possible about each thing and then sound healing came into my life. The expansion of my awareness that humans are so much more than their physical bodies became mind-blowing with this new idea of frequency! I was, and I am still in a constant state of awe every day.

Those first years were exciting and super challenging at the same time. As I began practicing Reiki and working with crystal singing bowls I really didn't have much guidance. There was a manual from the Reiki Institute that covered history and hand positions, but it didn't tell me about the personal clearing work that needed to come first. The hand positions were there to help us guide the healing energy, but they did not explain how to deal with the emotional traumas that came up during the releases in the sessions. In addition, I had just started dating someone that introduced me to the electronic music scene and all the parties and drugs that came along with it. The Universe had brought me Reiki and Ecstasy (the drug) at the same time and asked me to choose. I chose healing work and it was challenging to let go of that party life. I would get lost in the rhythm and the beat of the music for hours on the dance floor. The drugs intensified everything bringing me into a completely different state of mind and altering my experience as well. However, what I began to realize while experimenting with drugs and sober meditation, is that I could reach the same levels of ecstasy while sober, it just took a little longer sometimes. Once I got to that space, the reward, the feeling was even more valued. I was coming from many years of partying and this way of living and it seemed like this habit was "too hard" to let go of until a new friend, teacher entered my world.

When Troy Bunnell came into my life in 2011, I had just returned from four months of living in Mexico. I had left my last high-tech job, cashed in my 401K, started collecting unemployment and signed up for massage school. Everyone I knew thought I had lost my mind, but the move to Mexico was to help me decide whether I wanted to start my healing practice there or at home in San Jose, CA. I had been traveling through Mexico on and off for fifteen years at that point and dreamed of living there, so when the opportunity arrived, I took it. In the end, it was very clear that I was to build my healing practice in San Jose and then bring people to experience themselves in the energies of Mexico. Troy would be the one to catalyze the idea of me guiding retreats after I began studying with him and attending one of his "Power Journeys" in Tulum, Mexico.

Troy had studied the works of Carlos Castaneda and could recite passages from all of his books. He worked with Don Miguel Ruiz, the author of "The Four Agreements" and shared his modern view of Toltec Wisdom. Troy also worked with guided meditation and shared all the concepts he had gathered over the years of his awakening in the most loving and unconditional way. He introduced me to the works of Louise Hay as well. Troy was the main person at that time who challenged me to truly be myself and love every part of me on the journey of self-awareness. What most people don't realize about self-awareness is that it is also a practice of looking at the shit story you've been telling your whole life and then choosing to tell a new, more loving story. In addition, most of us humans don't know how to change the story because we've been telling it for so long. On top of that, it seems even more challenging when we do become aware of the shit story not to judge it or ourselves. The simple tools that Troy shared allowed me to see clearly how to work with my mind in changing the patterns that I was practicing, one thought at a time.

In order to change the patterns of anger, unworthiness and grief that I was practicing I had to show up and do the work each day. Meaning, I had to stop in the moment of the unloving thought and acknowledge it before I could let anything go. This simple practice of acknowledging and welcoming my feelings was a whole new thing for me. As I attended Troy's mastery classes each year, for three years, I started to understand how this simple shift in my thinking was actually super powerful in my transformation and healing. Just like Mike Dooley would say, "Thoughts become things… choose the good ones". I was starting to see the power behind our beliefs. I was seeing clearly that I had a choice, I just had to choose what felt more loving in the moment and that is easier said than done sometimes.

I will tell you now, there are NO short cuts in this personal clearing work. We must dig deep and look beneath the surface of our experiences to see why we choose to feel or react in certain ways. The emotional baggage that people carry with them is debilitating on all levels: mental, emotional, physical and energetic. It is important to be aware of all aspects as we let go of the limiting beliefs and stories we are telling. As I continued to practice acknowledging myself and my feelings, another simple tool I was introduced to was "the recapitulation" exercise or what I like to call "cutting of the cords". This is a practice of letting go of the attachment to people, places, and experiences that no longer serve us. It is a practice of Forgiveness. While working with this tool, I started to understand that visualization is really key in order for this movement of energy and thoughts to have an impact in changing our lives and physical environment. Visualization did not mean much to me before becoming aware of these ways of clearing my Self of old hurts and wounding. I attended workshops and worked with other teachers, but not until years later when I learned a little more about how our brains work did I really see how important our internal sight can be.

I attended a Joe Dispenza workshop in 2017 and really understood for the first time that the brain doesn't know the difference between what we see with our eyes closed and what we see when they're open. I had already been working with the imagination in healing, but when I pondered this in a new way, it took my curiosity and creativity to a whole other level. I began working with more guided meditations and leading clients on a journey with words weaved into my sound healing sessions. I started to sit in quiet meditation more often, visualizing and dropping into my dreams. I began noticing things manifesting into my world at a fast pace and even feeling overwhelmed by it at times. Things that I had been dreaming about for years were coming to fruition and way more amazing than I could have ever imagined. I also realized that we must be super clear in our intentions as we are in the creation process. Otherwise, we end up with a version of what we wanted and seeing how we can be more specific the next time around. I have found that sharing our dreams with others speeds up these manifestations as well. There is power in numbers!

For example, this book was just a bunch of thoughts in my head until I started talking to friends and mentors about it. I had already written many short pieces, I just needed to put them together and fill in the gaps. I also made sure to follow the synchronicities that were swirling around me, including when I had a conversation about my ideas with a dear friend (who is also a psychic and healer) and the very next day I received a "random" email from a person at Balboa Press saying they heard I was ready to publish my book. I took this moment as a very clear message that it was time to publish and that this was the way to do it. There are so many moments in my life that have seemingly happened "coincidentally" and yet the feeling of knowing that comes with them is undeniable for me. The magic that I experience on a daily basis truly amazes me! I imagine it will keep being more amazing as I continue to trust the flow of this life. I imagine it will be for You too as you practice the simple and profoundly transformative tools in this book. I highly recommend grounding in and creating your own safe space before practicing the tools in this book. Not sure how to do that? Read on.

INTRODUCTION

I am a firm believer in the power of our thoughts and the intention behind our words. I have always been a firm believer in being responsible for our actions as well. When we really consider that our actions come from the thoughts in our head, we are able to see that a thought and an action are one in the same. All of our actions come from a thought first. Whether it is conscious, or unconscious is another story. Most people are accustomed to looking outside of themselves to understand something happening in their life. In truth, all the answers are within each of us and these thoughts. If every person took a moment to be aware of the thoughts in the mind before acting or speaking, I know we would experience a lot less conflict in the world.

The simple tools and exercises in this book are here to support you in being aware of the unconscious and conscious thoughts and patterns that you might be practicing throughout the day. The first nine tools in this book may seem similar. They all have to do with introducing different ways of clearing your Self by working with the mind and the imagination. The tools are "repeated" in different ways, so that at some point the person is able to receive the message that allows them to move forward. I know the concepts and actions that I am suggesting in this book are not new. I'd like to specify that I don't believe we are learning anything new either. The ideas are simply being presented in a different way so that more and different people are able to take in the information. And, if you want to go one step further, I don't believe we are learning anything new at all in this life. I believe we are simply remembering what we already know innately within. I believe that learning is linear and implies we need time to understand something. I appreciate working with the concept of remembering more often because "remembering" for me implies "now" and can be known in the moment. Yes, we must make an effort and we can also allow information to flow to us easily as we remember. As you practice these exercises (impeccably) you will notice a difference in your experiences.

As I continue to work with these tools, I have discovered that as we practice them together intently, we are able to allow our Self and others their own experience without attachment. I see that I am able to let go of judgments in the mind more easily because I take a moment to observe myself and the thought. I am not saying that I never have a judgment, I am human. What I am saying is that it is easier to breathe and discern what is best when we observe. These tools allow me to let go of the labels "right" and "wrong" and accept what is in the present moment. I don't have to agree or resonate with it and I am able to allow it to be at the same time. Maybe it is beneficial to walk away in an intense moment in order to be conscious of my feelings. I give myself the space to do so by taking a moment and honoring or acknowledging my experience. I have found that I am able to be more clear in my thought process as I choose to observe my thoughts and feelings before responding in a situation that seems challenging. I do my best to be open to ALL options at ALL times.

In this process, I encourage you to become very aware of the words you choose to tell the story of you as well. Meaning, are the words I am speaking supportive and loving, or not?

Am I coming from a place of love, or not? Then, checking in and asking, "How does this make my heart feel?". Almost every human being is able to feel and know when they are in a loving space. Our bodies give us clear messages through experiences of dis-ease, pain and discomfort. Sometimes we ignore them or we just don't believe they are connected to the emotions we hold inside. As we practice observing and being aware of how we're feeling, as we are experiencing things, the easier it is to navigate any interaction in the most peaceful way. I recommend checking in with the unconscious thoughts in your head during your day to see clearly how you are participating energetically or have an awareness of your attitude towards life in the moment.

All throughout this self-exploration, the biggest message I have been compelled to share since the beginning of this healing journey is to BE grounded and to share information on what that means. I will remind you now that you are the writer, actor, director and producer of this play called "Your Life". You decide who you are in each moment and you choose how to react, or not. As you practice these tools and consider different perspectives you are allowing yourself to know You completely. As we choose to be aware of why we choose certain experiences, we reinforce our personal foundation and create our own sense of stability and security. We connect with our roots and support ourselves all on our own. We stop looking outside of us for validation and start asking our heart what we truly desire. To truly know your Self, is to LOVE your Self. Unconditionally! As you open yourself to all the opportunities life has for you, you will begin to see how synchronistic life really is and find yourself in a constant state of awe. I imagine the tools in this book will support you in achieving whatever state of being you desire.

Quote

Worthiness, in very simple terms, means I have found a way to let the energy reach me, the Energy that is natural, reach me. Worthiness, or unworthiness, is something that is pronounced upon you by you. You are the only one that can deem yourself worthy or unworthy. You are the only one who can love yourself into a state of allowing or hate yourself into a state of disallowing. There is not something wrong with you, nor is there something wrong with one who is not loving you. You are all just, in the moment, practicing the art of not allowing, or the art of resisting.

~ Abraham Hicks

TOOL #1:
CREATING SAFE SPACE IN THE MIND

As I began the journey of self-discovery and healing, I became aware that most people required a focal point to go back to in order to feel safe during their process. I also realized this is why working with Reiki was so resonant with me. The modality works with symbols that have a meaning to focus on when you are channeling the healing energy. If I noticed my mind wandering, I had a visual to come back to that allowed me to re-focus my attention. Symbols and visuals are powerful. We are able to bring the mind back to a particular place and time with them. We are able to connect with different aspects of ourselves. After working with the Reiki symbols for a while, I received a symbol of my own during meditation. I understood that it represented the idea of "as above, so below". I found that working with this visual allowed me to remain present with my clients more consistently. These symbols helped me to know how important creating safe space through visualization was for clients and other people. If you're interested in more information on the subject of Reiki, I highly recommend the *Reiki for Dummies* book. It is the most comprehensive and down-to-earth explanation I have come across.

I was about five years into my practice when a fellow energy worker asked me to do some sound healing for a client of hers while she was giving her a massage. The client was an older woman moving through cancer and chemotherapy. We were the only people in the studio that day. The space had the feeling of a log cabin in the woods. The room had nice berber carpet, a beautiful sage color on the walls and the heat was on so it was nice and warm. It reminded me of the cabin that my family had when I was growing up. It felt familiar and welcoming. I set up on the floor in the corner of the room and then waited outside for the client to undress and get on the massage table. When my friend and I entered, we turned the lights down low, so it was almost dark. My friend started the massage and I began playing some crystal singing bowls. After about five minutes, the client asked me to stop playing. She said that the sounds were scaring her and taking her into a dark place. My initial reaction was to encourage her to breathe with the sounds and to let go of the fear with the breath. I also felt myself wanting to argue with her. At this point, a little voice in my head suggested I just leave the room gracefully, so I did.

I left the massage room and sat on the sofa outside the door. I had a whole hour to sit there and wait to retrieve my instruments. I felt irritated at first. Then, I realized that I could still be of assistance. So, I began to envision a bubble of healing light around the client and an arch of healing energy between my friend and I as she continued to work with the woman. I focused on holding that vision for the remaining time of the session. When the massage was over, the client shared that there were no "hard feelings", only that the sounds were bringing her into some dark places in her mind and she didn't know how to get out of them. My friend and I listened to her story intently, gave her a hug and said goodbye. After she left, we sat together and talked about what happened and what could we do different next time. The first thing that came up was to create space with the client in their mind to give them a safe place to come back to if the mind wandered into fear. Meaning, verbally guide them in creating that safe visual space in their mind. Since that day, I begin and end every session with a guided meditation to create safe space in the mind.

EXERCISE: CREATING FOCAL POINTS FOR THE MIND

I recommend sitting in a comfortable chair that you have intentionally set aside for meditation. When we create a space with intention, the mind becomes trained to know that space for that purpose. We talk about this a little later in TOOL #3. You can also practice doing this in bed before you sleep at night. It all depends on whether you would like to do conscious or dreamtime work.

It is best to begin this work by grounding ourselves. I suggest working with the image of what it would look like for you to have tree roots growing out of the bottom of your feet. Maybe you're a tall and wise oak tree? Maybe, you are able to imagine what it would feel like as well? Are your roots thick and strong? See them deeply connecting you into the core of the earth and feel the connection in your body. You are welcome to work with this visual or create something that works best for you. Do your best to feel yourself grounded and connected to a foundation of some sort.

Begin by taking some deep breaths, in through your nose and out through your mouth. Maybe you count the breath in for 7 counts, hold the breath for 7 counts, and then breathe out for 7 counts. Do this for a few minutes as your body and mind relax.

On the breath out, imagine in your mind what it would look like for all the negative, unloving thoughts to leave the body with that breath out. On the breath in, imagine a beautiful white healing light entering your body at the toes and working its way up to the top of your head. Imagine the warmth of the light and how it would feel moving through your body. Part by part, organ by organ, moving through the blood in your veins and touching every cell of your BEing. Breathing it in more and more each time.

Once you have filled the body with white light, imagine your own light, your own picture of unconditional love. The picture can be of anything, there is no "right" or "wrong". Simply allow your mind to show you the first thing that reminds you of this love and place it in your heart. Imagine the picture in your heart center and feel the warmth of the love there.

Then, in your mind's eye, create a bubble around you. Imagine one of those soap bubbles from the little plastic jars with the wand in it. Allow yourself to see the beautiful effervescent blue, pink and gold colors swirling around you as you look out from inside the bubble. Feel the warm, soft, inviting space surrounding you. A safe and sacred space that you create in your mind. Invite your mind to be there with you and to allow everything outside to be in existence while your focus remains within the bubble. Allowing inside and outside to exist in harmony.

I encourage you to practice being in this space as you enter into your meditation, or quiet time with your Self. Once we give the mind a safe place to hang out, we are able to peel back more layers of emotions without fear because we have a focal point to return our attention. I invite you to practice this meditation and create your own as you hone your skills.

Quote

Our language is the reflection of ourselves. A language is an exact reflection of the character and growth of its speakers.

~ Cesar Chavez

TOOL #2:
SHIFT YOUR LANGUAGE AND PERSPECTIVE

Over many years of working with others and myself to hone my practice, I notice that my listening skills are a bit different than most people during a conversation. Now, I sometimes find it challenging to simply listen to a person's story instead of seeing the energy behind the words. The words and the energy behind them provide insight into how a person is feeling about themselves or what is occurring around them. When we become aware of the words we choose and why, we are able to see a different perspective as we feel into them. For example, when someone works with the statement "I am struggling" I don't feel like this is a very loving story to tell. And, I believe the energy of these words has an effect on the overall experience. By feeling into the words, we allow ourselves to see how we might be projecting out into the world. Maybe we work with the story of "challenge and an opportunity" instead of "struggle"? As we are able to be more aware of our intentions while speaking, we are able to shift out of any unloving thoughts that may be attracting something, or someone that does not resonate. The issue most of us encounter is that we are unaware when there is negative self-talk going on in the unconscious mind. When this happens, we don't connect that we may be matching the vibration of those thoughts that create our physical environment.

As we choose to observe the energy behind the words, or how it feels in our body, we allow ourselves to see the patterns that we might be practicing. I do my best to stay away from the labels "good" and "bad" or "right" and "wrong" when listening and if I hear someone working with these words it gives me insight into their story. As I work with a client, I choose to work with "loving" or "unloving" as the only labels in order to release the attachment of the many others that society places on us. I believe that most humans are able to know when they are coming from a place of love, or not, in any situation. If we do our best to stay in a loving state of being, it makes it easier to let go of the attachments to the negative thoughts we can carry about ourselves and others in the mind. Humans have thousands of thoughts per day and are only able to be aware of a portion of them. What are the other unconscious thoughts doing in there? And, if thoughts are what create our environment, and I look at the world today, I imagine many people are having some pretty fearful views of this life. I feel like we are being asked to be more aware of the unconscious mind now so that we are able to create a more loving experience in our entire community around the globe.

There are many words that we work with in our conversations that limit us in our experience daily as well. Some people may call it semantics, but I know how I feel when I hear someone working with unloving words in their story. For example, what if someone said, "I love you so much, but you are really challenging at times". I feel like a person may not be able to hear the loving words shared once the "but" and the negative comment come in. It might even feel like someone is pointing the finger at them by saying "you" as well. The moment we say "but", we have totally negated the sentence before that word.

When we are able to work with the word "and" instead of "but" we are able to validate and express a possible negative feeling at the same time. One could consider saying, "I love you so much "and" I feel challenged in our relationship at times". When we rephrase the sentence in this way, we take out the blame and share it without making it personal. For me this feels more constructive and it allows a person to express exactly how they're feeling from the most loving space. The other person still may not like what you have to say, and a person can know that they did their best to communicate clearly. It is also beneficial to check in with your unconscious thoughts to see if they were in alignment with what you "thought" were loving words coming out of your mouth.

Whenever I hear people working with the words "trying" and "thinking", I ask them to consider working with different words like "doing" and "being". It is helpful to work with statements like "I am" or "I feel" or even "I know" in order to tell a supportive story of the self. These statements allow us to take ownership of what we're talking about too. When I hear a person use the word "trying" over and over again, I see them being in the energy of simply "trying", but never "doing" anything they're planning to do. I see "trying" as neither "doing" nor "being". The person simply continues to "try" to accomplish their goals, instead of choosing to work towards them. The pattern of "trying" is common. I imagine after reading this you will become very aware when you use this word in the future. When you are aware of it, stop and observe how that story might be true and if there is a possibility to change it.

The word "thinking" for me seems to keep people in the mind and the mind is where the ego, or what I refer to as "the screaming voices" lives. In my experience these voices are not what we want to listen to when we are dealing with emotions. The voices in our head work well when we are solving math equations or driving our car, but when we're feeling through something it is beneficial to tap into what we are feeling in the body. Our bodies provide messages for us all the time, but most humans are not listening beyond the thoughts of the mind. The more we stay in the mind, the less we are able to pay attention to the feelings in our bodies. I find it equally important to be aware when we are making statements like, "I think I want to quit smoking" or "I think I want to start my own business" when setting goals. Why not just say, "I quit smoking" or "I am starting my own business"? It doesn't have to be the reality of the moment and a person can allow it to BE their Truth.

I have found that really owning the story with "I am" is so helpful in the manifestation process. For me, "I am" is the most powerful sentence in the English language. It is super beneficial to be conscious of the word you are putting at the end of that sentence as you're telling the story of You. One statement that seems to be controversial for people when I ask them to replace it is, "I am sorry". The subtle unloving connotation this phrase holds is actually really big when I step back and look at it. I don't see anyone as a "sorry" individual and when working with someone who is challenged they do not wish for us to feel "sorry" for them either. So why do we say, "I am sorry" when something goes "wrong"? I see us putting ourselves in the story of "sorry" and continually feeling sorry about something or someone. What if we worked with, "Please accept my apologies" or "I apologize" instead of owning the "state of sorry"? What if when someone died, we simply said, "I don't have any words, just know that I am here for you" or simply hug the person? Again, some people might call this semantics, but the more positive and loving words we choose to work with the more we create this environment in the mind, and it becomes the new habit or thought pattern.

Then, we come to the story of "facts" versus "truth" in this life. I see facts as something we think about and analyze. Truth for me is a feeling, a knowing, and is unique to each person. When a person is sitting in traffic, the fact is, there is traffic, and everyone is stuck in one place. The truth of the experience is how you perceive the "stuck" and what it means to you. Maybe the truth of this situation is experiencing being stuck and how to remain calm? Another truth may be the person seeing it as time alone with the Self and listening within. It really is all about our intention and perspective in each experience we choose. When we choose to feel the facts out to see if they're ours, we are able to discern our truth. My truth may be different from another person and both are correct. Being in our truth is asking ourselves to trust our feelings and intuition. It is asking ourselves to trust what we feel and create from that knowing space inside.

We are moving through a lot of facts throughout our day in different situations. The fact is, the story we're telling in the moment may not be the physical reality of the goal just yet. The truth is, as we choose to speak about a goal as if we've already achieved it, we are able to be there and experience it. As we practice more at being in this space in the mind and telling the story we desire to create, the easier it is to actually feel our way into the vision. In this process of becoming more aware of my energy, I see this difference more clearly as I observe myself in my interactions. The facts of a situation may be the "reality" at that point in time and it also doesn't have to be the final outcome. As we connect more with the messages of the body and how the heart feels, we allow ourselves to acknowledge what is true for us inside by feeling, instead of thinking.

For example, the fact may be that I do not have a million dollars in my bank account (yet), but the truth is, I am rich beyond my wildest dreams. The loving experiences we choose are the abundance we seek. Abundance shows up in many forms, not just as money. The facts we choose to see as our truth are usually taught to us by someone else when we are children. At some part of the journey, we are shown a different perspective that may show us a new way to move through life. Some people never choose to consider other options and that is perfect as well. However, when we simply choose to see another view point, we are allowing ourselves to see things in a new light. We allow ourselves to grow and evolve because we are not limiting ourselves to one belief or one way of being. When we are open to ALL options, we are able to release all feelings of resistance in any experience. We don't have to like the options or entertain them. We don't even have to agree on anything. By simply allowing ourselves to be open to the truth that each option is correct for someone on the planet, the easier it is for us to let go of control and allow it to be whatever it is for each individual. And as we release resistance from within, we allow ourselves to BE in a state of peace or non-resistance.

EXERCISE: TRYING AND THINKING OBSERVATION

Take a small piece of paper and write the words "trying" and "thinking" at the top of it. Carry the piece of paper with you and make a check mark next to the word if you find yourself using one of them. Acknowledge it, then replace it with and "I am" or "I feel" or "I know" in the sentence. As you practice doing this you will begin to tell a different story about your life. You will tell the story of a person creating and acting in alignment with their dreams instead of "trying" to manifest them. This exercise is one of the ways to be more aware of the unconscious thoughts about you, your experience and others. It also allows us to see the subtle energy behind our words and the effect it may have on our experiences.

Consider what you might be "trying" to accomplish, but it never gets done. Ask "why" you may be telling the story of "trying" instead of "doing". If someone is always "trying" to be a better person, but not actually being a better person, their experiences with others will reflect this pattern. Those experiences may be uncomfortable as well.

I guarantee from this point forward that you will be very aware anytime you choose to work with one of these words. You will notice a feeling in the body that may not resonate. This is the cue to go deeper into the "why" and see clearly what we may not be owning in the moment.

Quote

"If you really want to know how stubborn you are, just approach the idea of being *willing to change*. We all want to have our lives change, to have situations become better and easier, but *we* don't want to have to change. We would prefer that *they* change. In order to have this happen, *we must change inside*. We must change our way of thinking, change our way of speaking, change our way of expressing ourselves. Only then will the outer changes occur."

~ Louise Hay

TOOL #3:
RITUAL & MEDITATION

In all my years of practicing meditation and being quiet with my Self, I still experience challenges in going "there" to set the tone for the day. I am awake early every morning, but that does not mean I have the desire to get out of bed right away. I stretch a bit under the covers and the moment I move my two dogs jump up and get in. They are like little personal heaters and I love the cuddle time. I find it really difficult to want to get up and do anything, let alone meditate and stretch. It's also interesting to notice that sometimes when I am not meditating to start my day that the people I'm working with seem to be challenged by me asking them to practice this as a morning ritual. I laugh to myself when others mirror me, and I even share with them when it's appropriate. They hold me accountable for being impeccable in my practice. I see this as proof of how we are all so interconnected and present together on this journey. I am grateful for this accountability as well.

One book that I have found helpful in creating some structure with meditation and ritual is "The Abundance Book" by John Randolph Price. Since most people are looking to invite more abundance into their lives, I felt this to be a perfect example of how to start our day with a new perspective in quiet contemplation. Mr. Price practices Christianity and the book has a lot of references to the Bible in it, but for me the focus was on his unique way of seeing abundance. He may use the word "God" to describe what I call "Source Energy", and that may be perfect for you, but if not, do your best to let go of the labels and listen to the message. It has been eye opening for me each time that I've gone through the 40 days impeccably each morning. The true intention of the book is to be aware of our relationship with money, how we feel about it and in what energy we attract it. The book provides you ten different paragraphs to sit with in meditation for fifteen minutes. You are encouraged to sit longer the more you practice. After each meditation, you are asked to journal about what information came through for you. Most times what I wrote didn't have anything to do with the passage, but it was always revealing for me.

As I stated above, most of us desire to experience abundance, but never choose to do anything different in our daily routine. By making time to meditate or be aware of our thoughts, first thing in the morning, we are able to create our day in the mind. We are able to live in it there first. Remember, there is no "right" or "wrong" when it comes to meditating and if we begin our day by being aware in this space, we might provide ourselves a different way than "usual". I will also remind you that meditation is not only about sitting quietly with yourself. It is about being aware of these unconscious thoughts in a safe, non-judgmental space that you create in the mind while exploring these aspects of You. As we become more aware during our meditations, we are able to begin seeing the unconscious thoughts that are floating around in the brain. It is these unconscious thoughts that are the energy behind our experiences. I believe the vibration of these thoughts is what is creating our environment and if we're not happy with it, we absolutely have the power to change it with awareness and practice.

By creating a morning ritual with loving intention, we set the tone for our day. This time alone allows us space to ground ourselves and clear any energies (i.e. people, places, things) that no longer serve us. Simply taking a moment to allow the mind to bring whatever might not be serving anymore to our attention so that we are able to acknowledge it in order to let it go. Making time alone with ourselves is also a loving act of the Self. I find that practicing ways of loving myself is a really wonderful way to start each day. Even though things may not happen the way I imagined, by setting intentional goals each morning, or simply being aware of my energy (attitude) throughout my day, I am able to move through it with more grace, clarity and ease because I choose with awareness.

EXERCISE: CREATE AND PRACTICE A MORNING RITUAL AND MEDITATION SPACE

Create your own morning ritual and set the tone for your day. I recommend considering what you'd like to accomplish during your waking hours. This is also the perfect time to create what you desire through the imagination, guiding the mind with loving intention. A good time to see if we are directing or being directed by the brain. If you're looking for more structure, pick up a copy of "The Abundance Book" or find a book that resonates with you to follow to create your own version. I highly recommend free writing and journaling your desires and what you're creating within after meditating as well. Remember, there is no "right" or "wrong". It is also possible to work with this time to simply practice creating safe space in the mind as you discover what works best for you.

It is beneficial to create a physical meditation space with the intention of meditating. I have two intentional spaces. One is my yoga mat and the other is a beautiful, red velvet, antique chair in the corner of my room. The color red represents being grounded according to Vedic Healing and this tells my mind that's what it provides. I also have a little rug for under my feet and a pillow for my back as I sit to be comfortable. You are welcome to bring in candles, essential oils and gemstones to support your practice. And, I remind you that these objects do NO THING without your intention. BEing with the Self is a simple act. It does not need all the bells and whistles to make it work. Maybe listening to meditation music with earphones makes it easier to release distractions. I encourage you to do what feels best for you. It is also helpful to sit at the same time every morning, if possible, to create the new habit of making time for yourself.

Meditation does not have to be practiced only in the morning for it to be effective. I have found that making time first thing in the morning to set the tone helpful because I realize there are some unloving, unconscious thoughts in our heads most of the time. I encourage you to meditate sporadically throughout the day as well. Grounding into positive, loving thoughts and visions frequently allows us to remain in this energy. And if what we project is what we attract, I imagine this practice to be highly beneficial.

Quote

"Cutting energetic cords with others is an act of loving the Self. When we practice this method of letting go, we free ourselves of attachment to people and the outcome of any situation."

~ Jessica Neideffer

TOOL #4:
THE CUTTING OF THE CORDS

Cutting the cords with people and experiences is a technique that is super helpful for reclaiming our power in all aspects. Our personal evolution requires a substantial amount of energy, but many of us are constantly giving it to relationships with people, things, the places we live, and so on. Every place we have lived holds a vibration of us through our memories. When we move, our energy stays there unless we consciously withdraw it back to Self. We give our energy to our jobs and even the computer we focus on all day at work. When we are in an intimate relationship with another, we are completely corded in with them. They can pull energy from us at any time whether in the past, present or future. I believe our biggest energy leak is due to our emotional wounding and negative emotional charges from life experiences. Cutting the cords is a very powerful tool in releasing attachments to these traumas and people through intention and visualization. This clearing technique allows us to free ourselves from the belief that we are not able to move forward with grace and ease from any experience, no matter how uncomfortable or difficult it may seem. It allows us to see ourselves free in the mind which allows us to be free in the physical.

The technique of cutting the cords is less important than actually doing it. The process is best practiced sitting in a quiet place with the intention of going within like in meditation. If a quiet place is not available, do it anyway / anywhere so that you are acknowledging and releasing any unloving feelings in that present moment. When we practice this exercise, I see us lovingly taking back our power and lovingly giving others back their power. When we begin to love ourselves unconditionally, we realize that by allowing another to be in their power (even if they acted unloving) we are actually giving ourselves permission to be in ours. Really, when we practice loving unconditionally, we allow EVERYONE to be in their power. The act of "no conditions" allows all parties to move forward without attachment to the outcome. I am not saying that all parties are in agreement all the time. What I am saying is that the energy and the intention of "no conditions" allows for the ability to be non-attached to any situation.

This exercise assists us in taking back our power in a loving manner through an experience that we curate in the mind. When we visualize and ask the mind to cooperate in the cultivation of our desired outcome, we are allowing ourselves to feel it before it happens in the physical. Our thoughts are actually things, they are energy, and energy equals matter according to Einstein's theory of $E=mc2$. Think about it... What do we do first when we decide on something we want? We have an idea, we write it down, we design it, we share the thought, then it is manifested into this physical world. Working with this exercise, we can see our relationships clearly, how we wish them to be, and connect to the feeling of it through the vision. The mind is a powerful visual tool! We are able to direct our focus whenever we choose in the creation process. The issue most humans have while manifesting is that they are focusing on the things that don't feel good as they ask the

Universe to fulfill their desires. When this happens, we send mixed signals and only part of what we're dreaming can be delivered.

When we have exchanges with people (intimate or platonic) we connect energetically. In my mind, I see cords that look like an umbilical cord connecting us to the other person. These cords are energetic and can be seen in the mind's eye as we imagine them and where they might be located or connecting us to another. I see these cords transcending time and space, even if someone has died. If we have any unresolved emotional issues with them, the cords remain. Psychologically we may have healed and resolved a past relationship, but unless we intentionally release the cords, the relationship continues to hold us. If we have had a co-dependent relationship in the past, for example, the cords still affect our current relationships. We can also see how these cords tie us in physically with close family and friends when we have a strong desire to connect with them and they call us or send an email in the same moment. We can also see when we have a heated exchange with someone and we don't process the feelings that come up, we leave the moment still connected into the feelings of it and the other person(s). We leave the space physically, but the feelings and words stay with us long after the experience.

As we move on from these energetic exchanges, most of us are leaving them feeling depleted. Though some people are aware of how energy works and are mindful of clearing themselves, many people on this path are never able to create exactly what they desire. They are full of new age beliefs, but the person and their life hasn't really changed. They might be attracting more abundance, but still live in lack and pain because they have not cleared the old patterns or beliefs yet.

The person continues this way because they believe that if they understand this new concept, they have somehow grown. I assure you, they have not. There is really very little we need to understand as humans. The emotional clearing work must be done in order to create anew from a healthy foundation. Understanding is a by-product of doing the work. Understanding alone does not lead to growth. It simply allows us to see a different perspective and as we see differently, we are able to do differently, and this is how we change the pattern of giving our energy away to others.

Cutting the cords with someone with the intention of lovingly giving them back their power, gives the mind permission to BE non-attached to the outcome or person. When the mind connects with this awareness, it is able to move forward more easily because it sees us without the cords. It allows us to lovingly take back our power and move forward in what we are creating without attachment to the others' energy, beliefs, or thoughts. When I practice this exercise, I see the person I am feeling affected by in front of me in my mind. I also see any energetic cords that might be connecting us, and I cut them. I send that person back their energy cords with love and take back mine with love. I recommend practicing this in non-heated experiences with partners as well. Allowing yourself to be in a partnership with each person in their power, releasing the belief that we must be dependent on another to be successful or whole. We can also practice this technique with letting go of experiences, places, and things.

EXERCISE: CUT THE CORDS

To start, I recommend making a list of all the people that you feel corded into currently. You can make a list of the people you feel have wronged you as well. I suggest starting with the ones most present in your mind. In addition, make a list of everyone you have had sex with in the past and cut cords with them too. When we have sex with someone we are not only cording in emotionally, but physically as well. Remember, you don't have to cut this person out of your life. You can simply practice giving each person back their power with love so that each person may move forward in their respective lives. If you would like to let someone go from your life, that's fine. I recommend doing so with love so that the trauma you may have experienced with them is able to be dissolved.

Sit in a quiet place and work with the first person on your list. See them or imagine what they would look like standing in front of you in the mind's eye. Recall the memory that stands out the most with this person. Do your best to recall the scene and the sounds, smells and so on. Simply recall as much as you are able. As you cut these cords with intention, you will gain more clarity moving through the memories. The exercise also allows you to be non-attached to the person or experience.

Begin working with your inhalations as a tool of bringing back energy to your Self. As you breathe in, visualize yourself withdrawing your cords and energy from the person. You can also engage the physical body by using your fingers like scissors to cut the cords you see on your body through the mind's eye. Practice with each person for 5-10 mins to start, if the attachment feels strong.

Then, focus on your exhalation. As you breathe out, visualize yourself returning the other person's energy and cords to them. Work with a forceful breath if this feels necessary at first. Do this for about 5-10 minutes. Then, move on to the next person.

It may take several sittings to get through the people on your list, and you may find yourself coming back to a certain person. It's all perfect. Just go with the flow and what feels best for you in each moment.

Do this exercise however you see fit for you. Don't worry about the technique. Just see the person in front of you, cut the cords, breathe your power back into You, and then give the other person back their power with love. If you're not ready to give the other person back their power, then simply continue lovingly taking back your own. I also recommend reading up on Toltec Recapitulation and the Hawaiian tradition of Ho' Oponopono as you hone your skills of forgiveness, letting go, and allowing as you cultivate your own practice.

Remember... There is no "right" or "wrong" in the process.

Quote

My fascination with letting images repeat and repeat - or in film's case 'run on' - manifests my belief that we spend much of our lives seeing without observing.

~ Andy Warhol

TOOL #5:
THE PRACTICE OF BEING...
NON-ATTACHED

As I started practicing being non-attached in the space of the observer, I began to see the benefit of standing outside of myself at times during my interactions with other people. It allowed me to see clearly that if I had any attachment to the outcome of a situation, I was creating resistance within my body. As all of our 40 trillion cells vibrate the frequencies of our feelings out into the world, people and our environment respond to it. If I was not able to allow someone (in my mind) to have their own experience I would see situations become challenging because they were picking up on the resistance within me. When I stood outside of myself and watched the other person and I connect, it allowed me to observe the experience without the distractions of the feeling of any judgments coming up within my physical body. I was able to easily let go of any possible reactions because I was processing them before I automatically went into whatever feeling came first. I am not saying I am successful at this exercise every time, but I have noticed that the intensity and frequency of conflict in my life has lessened. This process allows us to be aware of these feelings and shift into something different and continue in the changing of the patterns that we practice.

As we begin to master being aware through the space of the observer, we see that it becomes easier to change our energy (attitude) and that there is no need to control an experience or the environment. The illusion of "control" is real in the mind, and for me, simply does not exist in the physical world when dealing with others. We can dream things. We can manage things in our life, but I don't believe we are ever truly in control of how anything shows up in our experience. What we are able to do is choose our reaction. I have also found that when I am open to ALL options in my experiences that I release all forms of resistance in my body. Meaning, when I change the feelings inside, I change the vibration that I am sending out into the world, which in turn makes it possible to change my environment. I don't have to like the option, entertain it, or do it. When I simply allow my mind to be open to it ALL, without judgments, I find that my experiences are much more fluid when I am not resisting.

I also realized that when I stepped out into the space of the Observer that I witnessed myself and others detaching from their feelings and disassociating from the experience. When I saw this, I became aware that the practice of being "non-attached" and "detached" are two different things in my observation. The intentions behind our words are powerful and I believe they create the environment around us. When a person is practicing being non-attached to a situation or a person, I see it as the individual choosing to observe instead of reacting or avoiding. When we are non-attached, it allows us to be part of any experience without feeling like we must do something or have the urge to change it. It really is most beneficial to allow each person their own experience and see every experience as correct for each individual. I see this practice of being non-attached allowing us to be present in the experience and giving others involved the freedom to be and do whatever feels best for them. We don't check out during the interaction, we simply see that it is not necessary to own or participate in another person's beliefs.

The definition of detached is "separate or disconnected". While non-attached has a similar meaning, it also relates to "not being concerned with material things". Simply choosing to not be concerned with someone else's "stuff" just makes life easier from a practical and logical stand point. I encourage you to practice working with both words and see how they feel to you instead of just using a word because it's comfortable. When we're out of our comfort zone, we're on the path of change. The journey of life is a series of decisions followed by the experience that comes after we make the decision. When we are ALL allowed to make decisions without judgment, it is easier to allow things to happen organically (even if we don't agree).

When we choose to be detached from anything in this life, I see it as a way of checking out instead of really letting go of the attachment to whatever or whoever it may be. When we check out, we are ignoring the feelings that we're experiencing in a situation. When we choose to ignore, we are not validating our feelings. If we don't choose to acknowledge our feelings, we will never be able to process and release them. The feelings continue to live on in the tissue and the cellular memory of the physical body. I see the vibration of these unloving feelings emitting from our bodies like beacons attracting the same experience with different characters as we remain in the same "vicious" cycle. We experience something that doesn't feel good in the body, but instead of observing it, we detach from it without asking why and it remains within us. The "why" is the answer to our question of how to change our experience, but most of us are not asking ourselves or listening to the answer coming from within. The physical body is always giving us clues to the "why" through the symptoms we experience at times. If we pay attention to these messages, instead of being a victim of the symptoms, we are able to see clearly how to move forward in the most beneficial way for our Self.

One of the most beneficial things we're able to do when we're in the "observer mode" is speak with clear intention. When we imagine ourselves outside of our body, observing our experience, we are able to be aware of the feelings coming up inside without being affected by them. We simply observe them. Through this observation, we can also see how we might be choosing certain experiences unknowingly through our vibration or attitude. What is the energy behind the thoughts and words escaping our mouths? Does the energy feel loving or unloving? What are we feeling in our physical body in the moment? Do the voices in our head match the voice in our heart? When we stop to ask ourselves these questions during our interactions, it allows us the opportunity to choose how we react, or not at all. It is much easier to see things clearly when we are non-attached emotionally to the outcome.

EXERCISE: THE OBSERVER

When I guide a person through this meditation of connecting with their Observer, I ask them to sit comfortably in a chair with their eyes closed and their feet flat on the floor. We begin by breathing deeply together, in through the nose and out through the mouth. I ask the person to imagine roots growing from the bottom of their feet connecting them deep into the core of the earth. Next, we breathe light into our body and create safe space around the Self. Then, we focus in on the tip of the nose to practice being aware of a specific part or aspect of ourselves. Then, we move to the heart center and bring all of our attention there. We become aware of the beating of the heart and the rhythm or frequency of our Self.

Once in this space, I ask the person to invite their Observer or Higher Self to show itself in the mind's eye. We now imagine what it would look like for your higher self to enter the mind and the room. We also remember that our Observer Self may not show up looking exactly like we look now and that it is not "right" or "wrong" how it shows up. It is simply the process of giving the mind a focal point and a space to move out into as you observe yourself in the current physical experience.

Once the picture of the observer is in the mind's eye, we simply be present with this version of ourselves. As we become familiar with this aspect of us, we then move into the space of the observer to observe ourselves from outside the body. As we view ourselves from the outside, we are able to view any emotions or thoughts coming up in our body and mind without reaction. We simply observe because that is all the observer ever does. There is no judgment or criticism involved and this allows a person to be still and choose how they respond in an uncomfortable situation from a grounded state of being.

The practice works for a person in their alone time as well. It is powerful to witness ourselves and acknowledge our feelings. When we are able to be aware of the feelings coming up within us, we give ourselves a choice in how we move forward instead of just reacting.

Quote

"At a certain point, you have to decide whether you'd be satisfied always acknowledging the beauty and greatness of what other people create or if you want to be in the same arena."

~ Kerry James Marshall

TOOL #6:
LET GO OF UNLOVING FEELINGS

The simple act of acknowledging our Self seems to actually be a very difficult task for most human beings. I am not talking about boasting or bragging. I am referring to acknowledging our feelings and the experiences that accompany them. For so long we have been taught to be in control of our emotions and not to share if it might upset someone else. Many of the people I work with have experienced parents that believe children are better seen than heard which can lead a person to believe they are not worthy of sharing their thoughts. Most people are practicing some form of this pattern of not feeling "good enough" and I see it keeping us all from being in our highest potentials. These beliefs can lead us into feelings of insecurity and a lack of confidence in the way we choose to be or how we choose to create in this world. When we acknowledge ourselves, we are validating the Self without looking outside for someone to do it for us… and this is a loving act of Self.

Acknowledgment is only the first step in this process of awareness. If we are able to practice this simple exercise, it is possible to accelerate the release of beliefs that are no longer serving us in order to create new thought patterns. For example, if someone is practicing the pattern of victim over many years, I see the possibility of this pattern being projected into the person's experience. If the person is not aware they are in this state of being, they may be attracting undesired situations or people into their life through this internal frequency or belief. This is not to say that anyone deserves to be harmed or abused in anyway. It is saying that the more aware we are of our internal dialogue, the more opportunity we have to change it if it no longer serves us. And, in changing the focus we are able to change the response and our environment. If in the moment of awareness, we acknowledge that feeling coming up and say out loud or quietly inside, "I acknowledge that I am feeling unworthy, unloved, unapproved of" or whatever it may be, we are changing the usual pattern of going in to the unloving belief that might be limiting us from moving forward differently.

What I understand about the process of seeing clearly and acknowledging how we're being at any given moment, is that most people are not very welcoming of their feelings if they are unloving. Most of us tend to judge the negative emotions instead of simply observing them as part of our experience. As we validate (love) ourselves by acknowledging our feelings it is also beneficial to welcome ALL the feelings because ALL of our feelings are valid. Even the ones that don't feel "good". If we only say that some are ok, we are saying that some part of us is "not good enough" and continue to perpetuate this experience in our life through the belief we are carrying. Remember, feelings flow and emotions are the feelings that get stuck or that we choose to hold onto. Validating our own feelings allows us to discern what is serving and what is not. When we welcome ALL of them, we release resistance from our being which brings us into a state of allowing. And from this state of allowing we will attract more of the same.

Another important part of letting go of emotions is through our breath. As it is, people do not really pay attention to their breathing throughout the day let alone work with it intentionally. Thank goodness our brain and body take care of making sure this happens even if the breaths are shallow. Once we become aware and welcome the feelings to release, it is helpful to imagine what they might look like leaving the body with the breath. If we give the brain a focal point in the process, we engage it and begin directing the experience instead of remaining in autopilot and following the body. As we practice breathing deeply more often during our day, we create a new habit of breathing with intention. We are able to work with the intention to flow our feelings out of the body before we respond in some unloving manner to a situation. We take a moment to pause and observe ourselves as we're breathing and become aware of the words remaining inside a little longer until we shift, or we choose not to speak them at all. Taking a breath gives us an opportunity to come from a place of love, every time. Imagine how different the world would BE if we all practiced breathing instead of reacting in the moment.

EXERCISE: ACKNOWLEDGE | WELCOME | BREATHE | RELEASE (AWBR)

This is a conversation I have with my Self throughout my day. I encourage you to talk to your Self more often and to have loving dialogue. Most of us are caught up in the negative thoughts floating around in our head. When we make the time to do something different, like acknowledge ourselves, we change this habit and begin working with loving thoughts more often. This tool can be used for present moment and past experiences as well.

Jessica Neideffer

Acknowledge

Any time you become aware of an unloving feeling coming up take a moment to simply acknowledge it in the mind. Say to yourself or out loud, "I acknowledge I am feeling sad, angry, frustrated" whatever it is and be present with the feeling. There is no need to judge or criticize it. By being aware and acknowledging the feeling you are validating the experience. The more you practice acknowledging instead of reacting, you begin to create a new habit as you change the usual pattern or neuropathway.

Welcome

The second part of the process is inviting the feeling up, sitting with it for a moment and really being OK with it. Remember, light can not exist without the dark. Welcoming it up allows you to accept things exactly as they are without judgment of the shadow parts of the Self. This allows for easy release because you have chosen to embrace every aspect of that present moment and the present moment is where we have the power of choice.

Breathe

Take a deep breath through the nose and release through the mouth. I usually breathe 3 times as it represents full circle (mind, body, spirit) for me. Breath is our connection to life. It is useful as we work with the visualization of letting go of the unloving feeling. Be aware of your breath throughout the day. Do you find yourself holding your breath sometimes? Check in occasionally and take some deep breaths to cleanse your body occasionally.

38

Release

Work with visualization of this belief being released from your being to engage the mind in a positive, loving thought or picture of what that looks like. Now the mind and the heart are on the same page working in alignment of letting go.

Also check in and see what story is being told in your head at any given moment during your day. Are the thoughts loving or unloving? How does the thought make your heart feel? This exercise will help you to be a master of your thoughts which will lead you to BE a Master of Intentional interactions.

PS… Tell a new story if the one in your head doesn't feel good. Tell the new story until it becomes your life. You can also work with TOOL #2 to see clearly how to create this new story by intentionally choosing your language.

Quote

"See if you can catch yourself complaining in either speech or thought, about a situation you find yourself in, what other people do or say, your surroundings, your life situation, even the weather. To complain is always non-acceptance to what is. It invariably carries an unconscious negative charge. When you complain, you make yourself a victim. Leave the situation or accept it. All else is madness."

~ Eckhart Tolle

TOOL #7:
AWARENESS OF THE ROLES WE CHOOSE

The human mind is a very powerful tool. We are capable of creating whatever we dream in this beautiful space with intention, focus, faith and trust. I have found that most people are creating exactly what they are focusing on, it just happens to be connected to the things that they perceive as "wrong" or the things that they don't have yet. I consider myself to be a pretty aware individual and yet I still catch myself seeing the negative instead of simply observing the situation at times. My dad (Joe) always reminded me that I had nothing to fear when I was out in the world and that it is beneficial to be aware of my surroundings at the same time. He simply asked that I be aware, he didn't mention it wasn't necessary to judge the experience. I didn't see the benefit in that until much later in life. Along with the judgments came the feeling of the victim occasionally. And if we want to go one step further, I realized how "self-important" I was being while in that state of judgment. Judgment does not allow for each to BE in his own.

I always do my best to take responsibility and acknowledge myself if I am judging something or someone. I find that the evolution of our awareness depends on being in these unloving states at times. You might say that I am judging "being judgmental" by saying it is "unloving" and you would be correct. This is from my perspective and this is all I am here to provide, a different perspective, from my own experience. There is no need for you to agree with me. I also know that when we are coming from a place of love, we get a much different reaction from others than when we are in a place of judgment. I believe it is possible to provide observations from a loving space so that people are able to hear the information we're sharing with them. It is always helpful to be conscious of the words we're choosing to speak. It is even more powerful when we are aware of the intention or energy behind those words so that we are able to change them and our experience.

When we are choosing to be in a state of judgment, we are saying that we know better. We might be saying that the other person is wrong, stupid, or a jerk. We might also be assuming that our ideas serve someone in a more beneficial way. The fact is, our idea or way of doing something may be more efficient. The truth is, there are many ways of doing things and moving through life. I believe there truly is no "right" or "wrong" in the decisions we make individually or as a collective. When you take away the labels, life is simply a series of decisions and the experiences that follow. Sometimes, those decisions lead us into experiences that don't feel very loving. I see this as the opportunity to shift back into the heart and listen. I like to ask myself, "How does this make my heart feel?" as I process through the feelings that come from the experience. When I ask this question, I give myself a moment to observe instead of reacting.

For example, in the past I was quite familiar with the pattern of judgment in the form of road rage while driving my car. By practicing this exercise of observing and asking how the heart feels, it allowed me to be aware and manage the thoughts in my head. Like the "fact" that I knew how to drive better than other people on the road. While the "truth" is, we all drive perfectly with what we know. The exercise allowed me to change my experience of driving from angry to peaceful by shifting this perspective. As we become more aware of the random thoughts in our head, the more opportunities we have to shift or change out of them if we find they are unloving. Most of us are judging or being the victim at some point throughout our day. Whether we verbalize it or not, we can place ourselves in an unloving energetic space of self-importance. From this space, I see us sending out the vibration of the belief that we know better than another on this journey. If we have an "attitude" with someone because we "think" we know better, we usually get a similar reaction mirrored back to us. When we choose these unloving ways of being or thoughts, people pick up on that feeling, not necessarily the words coming out of our mouth. It is helpful to practice being aware of this internal dialogue while we are speaking out loud to be sure we are clear in our communications.

EXERCISE: THE JUDGE & VICTIM

For the next week, keep a small piece of paper with you that has two columns on it. One column is titled "judge" and the other is "victim". Anytime you become aware of yourself being one or the other make a simple notation of it in the appropriate column. The exercise is to help us be aware of the role we're playing throughout our day. When we are aware, we have choice, and with choice, we are able to change how we react, and change the experiences in our life. We give our Self the opportunity to move out of victim mentality and BE in our power. We give our Self the opportunity to move out

Jessica Neideffer

of judgments and allow ourselves to experience the peace in letting go.

This exercise is not meant to make us feel bad about being the judge or victim. It is a simple guide to work with to BE more aware of the stories we tell about the Self that may be limiting us or attracting undesired experiences.

Quote

"Ego is obsessed with the outer experiences. Mastery is Being the Master of our experience at the source of it."

~Matthew Engelhart

TOOL #8:
LET GO OF LABELS AND EXPECTATIONS

A mentor and dear friend used to say that there are only two stories in this life. There is the story of love and there is the story of fear. Human beings are coming from one of these places at all times. When he shared this with me years ago, it resonated deeply and makes even more sense to me today. By only working with these two labels it allowed me to simplify and drill down to what was beneath my initial emotion or reaction and see why. I see love as an umbrella for all the things that feel "good" in the body. It is the space where all the labels of love, live. I am referring to labels like: forgiveness, compassion, worthiness, kindness, etc. I see fear as the umbrella for all the things that we experience that don't feel good in the body, like: anger, resentment, unworthiness, greed, or the belief in lack. While being aware of what we're choosing to feel we want to acknowledge all the feelings coming up because they are all valid. It is also beneficial to simply see if we are coming from a place of love, or not in any experience.

When we work with this method, we are able to quickly shift out of unloving feelings if we find ourselves in an uncomfortable situation. We must look at ourselves first, every time though. In my daily practice I do my best to acknowledge all the feelings coming up as I am experiencing them. I am able to see what space I'm in energetically or what my attitude might be by paying attention to the reaction I'm receiving from the outside world. All of us have had a heated exchange at one time or another and most of us point the finger outward at first. There is nothing "wrong" with this response. I believe that ALL options are correct. At the same time, we can allow ourselves to be conscious of whether it feels "good" within the body, or not. The body will tell you where you're at every time. Meaning, if your chest is tightening or your guts are churning you might not be coming from a place of love. These symptoms in the body are the cue to check in with the "screaming voices" in the head to see clearly where you're coming from in that moment. Remember, we will always catch more bees with honey, than with vinegar. It is helpful to be conscious that the words flowing from your mouth are in alignment with the loving voices of the heart, not the screaming voices in the head. It is also helpful to be aware that even if the words coming from your mouth seem sweet, if the voices in the head are not matching, the person on the receiving end is feeling the intention of the thoughts behind those words, first. Our words and thoughts must be in alignment in order to keep from sending mixed signals when sharing information.

When choosing love, over fear, I also find it helpful to be aware that the stories we tell in each moment are mirrored back to us by those who surround us. I believe we are ALL mirrors of each other and if we are pointing our finger out at someone, we can be sure that we're pointing at our Self in some way as well. I see the people in our lives as reminders of what we're working on internally or emotionally. They are not there to "offend" us, they are there to show us that we might

48

be practicing unloving patterns like anger, fear, frustration or victim at times. They show us the things we might be holding onto in the cellular or muscle memory that may not be serving us anymore. None of these feelings are "wrong", they just might not be serving us anymore and another person may be there to show you that in the moment. When we become more aware through this method of seeing ourselves in others, it also allows the possibility of letting go of the idea of separation. I believe that every human is born into love and is a loving being. I also know that we learn unloving behaviors through our life experiences and express them accordingly. I believe that part of our journey in this human body is to understand unloving feelings because when we leave this body we don't experience them. I see it as a privilege to get to move through challenges that allow us to be more connected to our feeling nature and that support us in listening more deeply to the messages from our physical body. I appreciate how each experience allows us to relate with others on a deeper level, cultivating trust and openness, fearlessly.

As I have become aware of unloving patterns in life, I realize that we also create attachments to these patterns through the labels we work with to tell our stories. I'm not just talking about the labels of the feelings we're experiencing, I am talking about labels like "mom" and "daughter" as well as "victim" and "survivor". For example, when I think of the label "mom" there are many expectations that seem to come with it, according to society. The expectations I had of my mom before becoming aware of this attachment were a tall order to fill. I expected her to help me learn how to deal with my emotions and assumed that she already knew how for herself. I expected her to cook me meals and keep a roof over my head. I expected her to be self-sufficient and not have expectations of me. I expected her to support and love me even if I was not being loving. I find these labels can lead us to many disappointments as we expect this person "mom" or "daughter" to do everything expected of them according to the outside view. And, if you really consider it, expectations will always lead to disappointment because we are assuming someone should do or be something other than they are in the first place. In addition, if we are able to consider the energetic view of a parent, we can see them as simply the portal that allowed a person to be here. If we are able to see the parent this way, then it might make it easier as an adult to let go of what we "think" they "should have been" for us in the limited mind.

And in our quest and vision as a collective to heal and evolve, I encourage people to consider letting go of the word "victim" in the description of their story all together. I have experienced rape and sexual assault and have never labeled myself a victim. Yes, it is beneficial to acknowledge the feeling of victim in the experience in order to process the trauma held within the body and mind. I also see it as beneficial to work with a different language as we move through the stages of healing and even choose to see ourselves as healed already as we tell this new story. If we are telling the story of "I am a victim", we continue to perpetuate this experience in our lives on a subconscious level. I see this subconscious belief carrying a vibration with it and people projecting the energy of this belief out into the atmosphere. We are all feeling beings. Most of us are able to feel when someone is sad or angry without them saying a word. When we become aware that a certain feeling is not serving us anymore and we choose to see ourselves differently by changing the narrative in our head, we begin to change the neuropathway we've been practicing to that point. As we practice doing this over and over, we create a new habit. As we are creating a new habit in our healing process, it is highly advantageous to work with energy healers, psychologists and massage therapists to support us in releasing the emotions held within. In my own healing, I have found all of these modalities to be helpful in choosing different ways of being in my life.

Finally, what if we considered letting go of all the labels and simply had experiences? What if there was no "good" or "bad" or "right" or "wrong"? It is not my intention to minimize anyone's experience of trauma or something "bad" happening to them. I see this option as a way for humans to tell a different and more supportive story of moving forward for themselves. If we are able to be open to ALL options, we are able to release any feelings of resistance within our Self. We allow ourselves to be in a constant state of allowing. We allow others to their experience without judgment. I am not condoning the harm of others or unloving forms of behavior. I am simply saying that we have the option to focus on the action of the other or focus on our Self and how we wish to move forward in the most loving way. Even if the other person does not choose the same.

EXERCISE: WRITE OUT LABELS AND PERSONAL MEANING

For the next week, pay attention to the labels you work with in your experiences to be aware of your thought patterns. Notice when you work with "good" or "bad" to describe situations or people. Check in to see why you might be labeling something or someone in a judgmental manner. Maybe, you consider what your expectations of "mom" and "dad" were when you were a kid? Do some free writing about the feelings that come up regarding the expectations you felt were not met as a child. Personally, I usually find something I didn't see before when I go back and read what I wrote. Do your best to leave judgment out of the process.

If the judge in your head pops in, work with TOOL #6 to let it go. I also suggest applying TOOL #4 and cut cords with whoever or whatever comes through while writing.

Quotes

"He who does not accept and respect those who want to reject life does not truly accept and respect life itself."

"Every act of conscious learning requires the willingness to suffer an injury to one's self-esteem. That is why young children, before they are aware of their own self-importance, learn so easily."

~ Thomas Szasz

TOOL #9:
AWARENESS & ERADICATION OF SELF–IMPORTANCE

Ahhhh… The subtle energy of "self-importance", we know each other well. This beautiful energy helps me to be aware when I am in a space of resistance. At times, it is a gentle reminder that quietly passes through my brain before action. At other times, it is projecting out of me into the atmosphere for all to experience. Most people feel that self-importance is a "bad" thing, but I see it as a valuable tool. It is a wonderful gauge I work with to see if I am being present in my interactions and decisions. While I do my best to stay in a more loving space energetically, I am grateful for the challenge this state of being provides to be more clear in my intentions. As we become more present with our feelings and thoughts, we give ourselves opportunities to do or think something different than we have been choosing to that point. As we become more aware of how we are being in the present moment, we give ourselves choice and an opportunity to change our experience of "self-importance".

For me, self-importance is an unloving state of being, not "bad", but maybe not serving anymore. I see it expressed in many forms and when I suggest to someone that they may be practicing this way of being, I get a similar response almost every time. The response is usually defensive and is followed by some denial or explanation. My experience is that no person really wants to acknowledge they are being unloving, including myself. I admit, this may be a "life lesson" for me (for most people) and what I notice is that the intensity and frequency of this belief coming up is lessening as I continue to be more aware of the thoughts in my head and how they feel in my body. Self-importance can show up as someone always being late or having one-sided conversations. It can show up in the way we put value on the material things we have accumulated, like the car we drive or the house we live in. I also see many of us placing so much emphasis on the job we have, how hard we work, and how much financial abundance we're able to attract. There is nothing "wrong" with having nice things or an abundance of money. I also see the benefit in being aware of "why" we put so much attention into these "things" that have nothing to do with who we truly are.

In my experience, the energy of self-importance is so subtle, that most of us are not even aware we're operating in this mode. I believe this is why it is so hard for us to admit to it sometimes. We really don't see it. Like when we're living in communal spaces with our family, friends or intimate partners. Each person has their idea of how they think the home should look and feel. Each person also believes their way is the "right" way. Then, there is some sort of compromise and working together to create the space. However, once the space is created and things are in their place, we then might start paying attention to making sure those things stay in their place. I have found myself moving things that are not mine because it looks and feels more esthetically pleasing to me. I have had housemates take down artwork and replace it while I was on vacation. I have come home to whole rooms in the house being painted without talking about the changes first. These are all ways of passively saying, "My way is better than yours" even though that person may see it as "doing you a favor".

In addition, I have experienced self-importance while working with executives and other administrators in high-tech companies. Whether it is co-workers sharing false information, saying it's not their job, or executives acting like prima-donnas and having unrealistic expectations, we are all practicing it to some extent. And if we're experiencing it with our co-workers, we might want to check our attitude to see if we are somehow projecting out the subtle energy of self-importance as well. I believe in the law of attraction and see life through the eyes of "what we project, is what we attract". So, if we are feeling like we are better than others or that our way is the best way, we might just be eliciting this experience, energetically with another. It is also possible to elicit a similar experience of self-importance if we are choosing to be in the mode of victim, possibly attracting the opposite energy of feeling important so that we are able to remember our worth. And, in the end, if we are practicing any form of self-importance, we have forgotten how worthy we truly are anyway.

One of the biggest ways self-importance has shown up in my life is tied to the "need to be right". Usually people want to be "right" because it makes them feel important or smart. If we look a little deeper, it's all about approval and feeling good enough. One of the people I shared a home with was a very intellectually smart human being who was also aware of spirit. Many of our discussions were about meditation and healing. I have many opinions and beliefs on this subject that I am passionate about and my way of expressing myself was not always received well by this person. I believed that I was right, and they believed they were right. And when you strip away everything, we are both correct. The need to be right on both sides became a small battle at home after a while and got to the point where I was having visions of physically hurting this person. I became tired of the "needing to be right" and really wanted all conversation with that person to end.

After a about a year of living together, I was ready for this person to move out. I started imagining our home as a harmonious space, even though that's not what it felt like when we were there together. I began imagining that we lived in a space that was loving and supportive. I kept my interactions with the person to a minimum to continue my focus on harmony. One day, I had a conversation with a good friend of mine about the experience. She laughed when I told her some of the conversations we were having and how I was having visions of punching this human in the face because I was allowing myself to feel so irritated. Not that I would ever harm anyone physically and if I'm having the thoughts often, and thoughts can become things, it may add to the manifestation of it actually happening in the physical. My friend reminded me that I was not being very loving with these thoughts and then asked me to close my eyes and go into that vision of hurting my housemate. So, I went there in my mind and saw the person with me. Then, before I even got to the physical part of the vision, she asked me to see the housemate as a five-year-old version of their self. My heart stopped for a moment as I witnessed me raising my hand to grab this 5-year-old in my vision. The vision was so real, it made me feel sick to my stomach.

In this moment, I could see clearly that adults are a bunch of wounded 5-year-olds running around in larger bodies. We are all seeking to be loved, approved of and accepted in our own unique way. In order to have compassion for people, we must come back to ourselves and ask why we are choosing to be affected by them. It is also helpful to consider what must have happened to that person for them to behave in a certain way. We must ask ourselves why we are part of the experience and how we could act differently. It all comes back to the Self and what we are choosing to feel at any given moment. I find it easier to let go of being right when I am able to see the small child in each of us. I now find myself wanting to hug people and tell them that everything is ok, just as I would do for a child that was hurting or seeking attention. I am not saying I am successful at this every time, but the intensity and frequency of unloving feelings of frustration have lessened with this practice.

EXERCISE: THE 5-YEAR OLD SELF

We all have at least one person that seems to be challenging in our life. I highly recommend beginning to see them as a young child during any interactions that bring up feelings of irritation, frustration, anger or anything else that feels unloving. Start cultivating compassion for this inner child. Most of us tend to let go of the need to be right when we are able to see the wounding of the other. Practice being aware of how the other person is feeling to you in the moment. It does not matter whether the person is physically present, or not. The exercise is powered by our intention and imagination and this is the space where we are able to create a new, loving story and then choose to live it.

Close your eyes and go back to the last experience you had with them. See the person as this young child seeking your love and acceptance. Remember how you felt in elementary school when you didn't feel accepted by the other kids. Maybe you go back to a time when you didn't feel that your parents were hearing you? Do your best to put yourself in the other person's shoes and really feel into their story instead of the "need to be right". Maybe you find that you are able to relate? When we relate, we create compassion, and this is what helps us to let go of that need to be right, which is the same as self-importance.

I also encourage you to do this exercise with your Self and give You permission to BE forgiven as well.

Quote

"The *human form* is a conglomerate of energy fields which exists in the universe, and which is related exclusively to human beings. Shamans call it the *human form* because those energy fields have been bent and contorted by a life-time of habits and misuse."

~ Carlos Castaneda

TOOL #10:
MIRROR WORK

Mirror Work is a very powerful tool to utilize while making changes in our way of being and living. We are constantly looking outside of ourselves for others to validate what we're doing, but we don't often stop to consider asking ourselves instead. Maybe we are able to hear the voices in our head, but what about looking our Self in the eyes and asking questions or giving validation on our own? We do this for our loved ones and colleagues, why wouldn't we do it for ourselves? When I first became aware that this was a thing, I thought it was ridiculous and even a little egotistical. The resistance I felt to looking deep into my eyes and saying, "I Love You, Jessica. I really, really love you" was so strong it made me super uncomfortable and curious at the same time. Why would I feel so repelled to say, "I Love You" to myself? I realized after I started having conversations with me in the mirror that I was afraid of the judgments coming from the screaming voices in my head and what others might think of me talking to myself. These voices had nothing loving to share with me and that was where the mirror came in. It reminded me that I was good enough to share this truth with my Self.

We have all been judged or criticized at one point or another in our lives. If people didn't care so much about what other people thought of them, we would not have so many problems in the world. However, most people tend to take things personal and hold onto the unloving words and feelings that are sometimes shared. These things become memories in the mind and are also carried at the cellular level. Some of us carry these beliefs for years not knowing the damage that the hurt or anger may be creating within our bodies. Because of this conditioning, we tend to do the same when we look at ourselves in the mirror. We are usually noticing or commenting on something that "we don't like" out of habit instead of seeing our qualities. What if we all started saying loving things to ourselves in the mirror regularly? What if we said, "I Love You" and stared deep into our own eyes the way we wish another to do with us?

It is integral as we become more aware to begin practicing looking ourselves in the eyes, in the mirror, to change these unloving beliefs. The first part of this exercise is simply being willing to consider a different way. Even if you only consider it, that is a start to changing any unloving patterns one might be practicing. Start making it a habit when you're getting ready in the morning, make it a ritual. Look at yourself in the mirror and say, "I am willing to consider something different". When you say this to yourself make sure you are looking deep into your eyes, not at the gray hair on your head or the blemish on your nose. Notice how you feel when you share positive and loving words with yourself. Notice any resistance to the words as well. Many people are not comfortable taking compliments from others because they don't believe it about themselves. If you feel resistance to change, ask yourself why. Maybe ask yourself what old belief you may be holding onto and free write about it? I find that having a deep, fact-to-face conversation and writing about it go hand-in-hand. We bring our thoughts into the physical when we put them on paper and when we're looking at ourselves in the mirror, we are adding the physical features to the voices in the mind.

While practicing getting to know You better on a different level, we can work with whatever mantra or new thought pattern that resonates. Simply being willing to consider hanging out with yourself in the mirror is a start. Begin by practicing looking yourself in the eyes and saying, "I Love You" and be aware of how you feel and where the sensation is showing up in the body. Maybe you practice the mantra "I am willing to release all resistance" and notice how you process that feeling if it comes up for you again? As we become more adept and comfortable in the practice of staring at ourselves, we can also start practicing the technique of "gazing" as we begin to connect on a deeper level.

When we "gaze" into our eyes, we lose focus and allow ourselves to see double like when we look cross eyed, but our eyes don't cross. As I began gazing at myself in the mirror my face started morphing and showing me what seemed to be shadows or other versions of my Self during my conversations. Yes, I realize this may sound out of the ordinary, but if you think about it, we have a bunch of stories going on in our head daily. If we choose to consciously tap into these stories, we are able to see which ones (or versions of our Self) may not be serving us anymore and let them go with awareness. The only way to truly release anything from our being is to be aware of it first. The mirror and the heart will always tell us the truth. For a really amazing example of mirror work, I recommend checking out Teal Swan on Youtube. She has a video called "The Connection Process" that is quite in depth. I also recommend working with mantras from Louise Hay's book "You Can Heal Your Life" until you begin to create your own. I guarantee you will begin to feel different about your Self immediately.

EXERCISE: MIRROR WORK

Make time each morning to speak to your Self lovingly in the mirror. Begin with this version of simply talking to yourself out loud and looking into your eyes. Notice how you are feeling in your body as you share. What sensations are arising and where? As you master this way of connecting with You venture out into other ways like "gazing" or seeing multiple versions of you. I like to work with one mirror in front of me and one behind sometimes, so I am able to create the affect that there are many mirrors and versions of me. I love how this technique supports us in seeing ourselves as the multi-dimensional beings that we are. Be playful when possible and open to whatever presents itself. The mirror provides an opportunity to see clearly how we wish to look and feel as we move forward in life.

Quote

"I can shake off everything as I write; my sorrows disappear, my courage is reborn."

~ Anne Frank

TOOL #11:
WRITE YOUR WAY TO FREEDOM

Writing is beneficial in any healing process and can be quite empowering as we move through life. Writing is expressing ourselves and bringing our feelings into the physical. Writing our dreams and goals down on paper can help us in creating and manifesting what we desire by giving us a focal point. It gives us something physical to look at, feel and touch. We can write to create, or we can write to let go and release what is no longer serving us. Writing letters or simply free writing allows us to say all the things we wish we could say in a safe environment. I believe writing gives us the courage to begin sharing our feelings with others in person as well. Writing provides a different way of seeing an experience. We are able to consider other perspectives of a situation more clearly when the thoughts in our head are on a piece of paper in front of us. When we give ourselves the opportunity (without judgment) to see what's going on inside, we allow ourselves to be present with those thoughts so that we can decide whether they serve us, or not. As we process those thoughts and feelings within, we become a master of them and more aware of the mind and the patterns we practice.

I attended a retreat once where we were asked to write our own eulogy as part of our clearing process. I laughed at this request and then proceeded to cry my eyes out when I read my eulogy in front of the group. We were asked to write from the perspective of the person that we felt loved us the most. The exercise brought me back to the concept of mirror work and how we are always willing to say loving things to others, but not ourselves. I see the process of writing our eulogy as giving us space and permission to see the many qualities we possess within. Just like in mirror work, we are practicing speaking to ourselves in a loving manner. How often do we leave love notes for our kids or significant others? We long for others to do this for us, why not do it for our Self as well? When we tell someone that we love them, we tend to feel loved just from sharing our feelings. When we validate ourselves, we release any belief that we need anyone to tell us that we are good enough. We choose to see ourselves in a different and maybe more loving way. I see the personal eulogy as a love letter to the death of our old ways and the birth of a new relationship with the Self.

We can also write letters to other people, dead or living. The letters can be angry, loving or both. We are able to write to someone who has died telling them all the loving things we didn't say when they were alive, or we can write angry letters about hurt feelings never expressed. An angry letter allows us to really see deep inside what we might be carrying around with us emotionally. Usually when people begin to write about these angry feelings, they become aware of thoughts they didn't know they had, and it surprises them. And, usually they are able to see that it is not really anger, but some underlying hurt or sadness. I encourage people to put in writing whatever comes up, no matter how "horrible" they think it might be. Remember, these letters are only for You. Write the most unloving, even hateful things to get them out of your head so you're able to see clearly where you're at energetically. I see this as sharing the feelings without harming anyone. There is no need to share these unloving thoughts with others, although the ego (the screaming voices in the head) might say otherwise. When we become aware of thoughts we didn't see before, it allows us to acknowledge something more, which allows us to peel back another layer of the Self and become even more clear in our thoughts.

As we move through this process, I feel it is important to burn letters that are releasing unloving feelings, people and things immediately after we are finished writing them. When we write something on paper and bring it into the physical, we are giving it life. If we are holding onto the letters of unloving feelings, we must ask ourselves why. If we are letting something go, the burning is the action that shows the mind we are finished with the person or thing connected to it. The intention of burning is to cleanse and purify whatever feelings or beliefs came up in the writing. For me personally, when I burn my letters, I always feel lighter and relieved. I feel a renewal and permission to move forward into something different.

Free writing is another release technique that allows us to be aware of the unconscious thoughts in our head and provide an opportunity to change or cultivate them. Free writing allows us the freedom to simply write without reason. I feel like it lets us "get out of the box" and gives us permission to do something different. I find it helpful to free write after meditation to see if I become aware of any new thoughts and ideas that might be floating around in my brain. I really appreciate the way this technique allows me to see clearly what might be holding me back at times. When we are able to see clearly it makes moving forward less intimidating. I highly recommend making time in the morning to journal after 15 minutes of being still with yourself. I encourage you to embrace all the thoughts and allow them to pass as you focus on being present with You. There is no need to repel any of them. Simply be aware and then give yourself some time to listen within and put it on paper. I guarantee you will have some revelations.

During this process of writing and being aware of the patterns we practice, we must remember to allow ourselves time to grieve as we change. We must allow ourselves time to process the loss that we might feel as we begin to practice new ways of being. The core of who we truly are remains the same and at the same time we are choosing something different to practice. We are releasing parts of who we thought we were. For example, the belief that we are unworthy or not good enough. I believe this is the issue for almost every human being on the planet. After practicing thoughts like this for many years, it only makes sense that we would feel a sense of loss, or even loss of identity as we choose different and more loving ways of BEing. Working with TOOL #6 to acknowledge any feelings coming up in your writing is helpful. I also recommend TOOL #4 to cut the cords with people in the letters.

EXERCISE: FREE AND INTENTIONAL WRITING

Choose one or more of the suggestions for writing above that resonates with what you're experiencing in life presently. If you're meditating and journaling, I suggest making this a morning or evening ritual so that you create a new habit. Remember, when we practice something new, we are able replace the old patterns no longer serving us.

If you choose to write a personal eulogy, I recommend keeping it to one page and write it with pen and paper. Write it from the perspective of the person you feel loves you the most in your life. And remember, there is no "right" or "wrong" in this process. The point of the exercise is to be comfortable writing loving things about yourself from the heart and cultivating that love in your physical world.

And… Remember to burn any letters written with the intention of releasing feelings no longer serving you immediately after your process. There is no need to hold onto the feelings or the person anymore. And if you find it seems challenging to burn right away, ask yourself why.

Quote

"The goal of the journey of life is to rise above the challenges of the human experience to be the embodiment of LOVE in the flesh."

~ Jessica Neideffer

TOOL #12:
REINTEGRATE OTHER VERSIONS OF THE SELF

There are different definitions of the idea of soul integration. Sometimes, people have a shaman or healer do it for them silently during a healing session. I have experienced that it is also beneficial for some people to have them participate in the process visually. I have found that guiding a person verbally and creating a landscape helps their mind to participate and follow as we create consciously. When there is intentional guidance, most people are able to let go of the "screaming voices" in the head and be truly present in the meditation. Remember, those voices are only good for solving math equations and driving your car. In addition, as a healing practitioner, it is helpful to feel as the person is moving through the meditation. It gives me a gauge to know where they're at in their process as I hold space while they clear.

Soul Integration for me, is a way of working with the mind to invite different aspects of our Self to return home to the heart. When we experience something traumatic in our lives, I believe we carry the memory of it in the cells of our body from the moment it occurred. It doesn't matter if it seems "big" or "small" it is remembered for a reason. The book, "The Body Keeps Score" by Bessel van der Kolk, talks about how important it is for people who have experienced trauma "to become familiar with and befriend the sensations in their bodies" in order to heal. In my experience, it is beneficial to connect with the version of our Self that incurred that trauma to see if there is any information they would like to share with us to support our healing. When we go into this space, it is not to relive a traumatic event, it is to have a simple conversation with this version of us. Some of the sensations connected to a trauma may surface and this process allows us to create a safe space in the mind to have the experience, first.

Visualization has been a key part in my healing process over the years. Visualizing with intention to let things and people go has been a powerful tool. A mentor of mine did this guided meditation with me and five other women. He guided us into the same visual space together and then asked us to ask this younger version of ourselves how they were feeling during that time of our life. I personally received some messages from my 15-year old self that weren't really new, but I felt like I heard them for the first time. I could really hear her answering my questions and I was able to see her sitting on a park bench with me under an old oak tree. I could even feel a breeze touch my cheek as it moved past me in the vision. I remember the experience being so visceral that I cried. And now, occasionally, I visit different versions of myself on my own when I have things come to my attention.

The practice of hanging out with our "Selfs" allows us to be aware of the feelings that might be hiding behind the scenes from certain experiences. The practice of reintegrating pieces of ourselves supports our time in meditation and honing our skills in visualizing desired outcomes. We practice listening to our true voice and trusting that what we're hearing within is absolutely real. Remember, the brain doesn't know the difference between what we experience with our eyes closed or open. Why not create and experience exactly as you desire in this space where anything is possible? In this space, we are able to hug our younger self and remind them that everything is ok. We are able to listen to them and act in the way we wished others to act with us when we were a kid. We are able to change the dialogue within by creating a new story for our Self. And, as we tell this new story, we begin to feel and act different in our experiences moving forward. We are able to let go of hurt feelings and beliefs that came from holding those hurts for so long.

As you practice the exercise below, it is beneficial to work with a healer to assist you in moving any stuck emotions or memories that you may not be aware of as you begin to understand how to clear your channel. It is helpful to have a guide through the process even when you are aware of what you're letting go.

EXERCISE: SOUL INTEGRATION

Create a quiet space to sit comfortably. Maybe you have some gentle meditation music on in the background or with headphones on? I recommend starting your meditation by grounding in and creating your bubble around you, like we talk about in TOOL #1 to create safe space.

Once you have created your space, you are then able to envision the scene where you will meet and chat with a younger version of yourself. I recommend making a list of the ages where you remember something that has stuck with you over the years. Ask yourself what age you remember it happening to give yourself the visual of you at that time. I suggest working with each of those versions of you in separate meditations to allow yourself to fully process.

You are welcome to create any back drop that feels best for you. Maybe it is in a park, sitting on a bench with your younger self? Maybe you are on a white sand, blue water beach somewhere tropical? See yourself and this version of you in a space that feels loving within. Visualize in detail what it looks like around you in the mind. Allow yourself to be present with everything in this vision and connect with the younger you. Feel your way into the space as you imagine it in the mind.

Ask this version of you to sit with you and share their feelings. Listen intently. Ask this version of you permission to share how you're feeling when they're finished sharing with you. You are also welcome to share with them all the things you wished others had shared with you in the past. Maybe you tell the story of the things you're most grateful for currently and in the past? Share with them that everything is ok and how grateful you are for them. Share how grateful you are for the experiences they had for you and how they allowed you to be who you are today. Express this gratitude in the most deep way you are able to imagine. Tell them how much you love them and remind them again that everything is ok. After sharing, ask permission to hug the younger you, to embrace yourself in this space in the mind. Tell this beautiful new story of love and understanding. Tell this new story of You.

Once you feel this process of sharing is complete, I invite you to then see this version of you shrink down and fit in the palm of your hand. Continuing with your eyes closed, as you sit in your chair, physically extend your left arm out in front of you so that you can see your hand in the mind's eye. See the younger you in the palm of your left hand. Maybe even feel the warmth from their tiny feet on your palm? Then, see a door in front of your heart opening into your chest. See your light shining out as the door to your heart opens. Take your hand and place this tiny version of you through the doorway and into your heart center. Return this version of you that may not have felt loved or accepted, home to the heart. Allow yourself to feel them in your heart space. Maybe you feel a warm sensation there? Allow yourself to know they are one with you and see yourself as complete and whole in the mind. Imagine what that looks like for you. Remember, there is no "right" or "wrong" in the process. Practice working in this space of change and creation to manifest the outcomes you desire. Remember, resolutions don't always have to be experienced in the physical world for them to be accepted in the mind.

Quote

"Let us remember that although to all outward appearances, music seems to be over as soon as the last chord has sounded, and the celebrants have dispersed, this is not the case. It has also been created on a subtle plane and remains like an exquisite flower hovering over the sanctuary. No musical vibrations are ever lost, even though they are dispersed, they will go on vibrating through the cosmos for eternity because the subtle effects of sound linger after the audible sound has died out, so that any results are long-lasting."

~ Renee Brodie

TOOL #13:
HEALING WITH SOUND

Sound Healing has been a part of my healing practice since 2007. This therapeutic modality resonates deeply with me and I am passionate about sharing it. I'm pretty sure that I knew this was "a thing" at a very young age as I look back on my life. I remember listening to my parent's records as a kid. I remember how songs like "The Dancing Bumble Bee" by Neil Diamond made me want to spin in circles in the living room until I would fall to the floor watching the world spin around me. I remember hearing Janis Joplin and Jimi Hendrix and feeling their music move through me like a breeze and how it gave me goosebumps. I remember the first time I heard Billie Holiday sing "Come rain or come shine" and how it made me cry. I was able to feel their passion through their songs. I have always felt that music is universal, and rhythm doesn't need words to be shared with and enjoyed by others. Through my own experiences with sound and music, I have found that I am able to connect with myself and others on a deeper, feeling level. When we work with sound as a focal point to join our bodies and minds in healing, it is possible to intentionally create a space of rest. And once the mind is at rest, the body is able to let go and allow the same. I believe it is in this space of deep rest that we heal.

In my practice, I work with instruments called crystal singing bowls. Each of the instruments plays a note on the musical scale (A thru G) and each of those notes is connected to different areas of the human body. The healing modality is based in the tradition of Ayurvedic Medicine. It suggests that each of these frequencies (played with intention) have the capacity to bring harmony back to the cells if we are experiencing an imbalance in our system. Since all the forty trillion cells we're made of are in a constant state of vibration, working with sound (vibration) to create harmony or homeostasis within makes sense to me. I have witnessed people regaining mobility in their physical limbs and chronic pain disappearing after one session. I have also experienced people being able to acknowledge and release old hurts with the sounds of the instruments and our intention. I have witnessed people let go of old behaviors and create new more loving experiences in their lives.

Western Medicine is already aware of the benefits of sound and how powerful it truly is. Ultrasound is worked with to dissolve kidney stones with frequencies to avoid surgery and to check the health of unborn babies. Recently, I became aware of Anthony Holland, a professor of music, who was invited to work with doctors to discover frequencies that dissolve cancer cells. Anthony's TedTalk from 2013 is now gaining attention for the studies that were conducted and a video showing cancer cells being shattered by sound under a microscope. Dr. Mitchell Gaynor was an oncologist that worked with people experiencing terminal cancer. He provided crystal singing bowls to his clients to assist them in their healing process during treatment. People who chose to work with the instruments along with their voice were able to live for years instead of weeks beyond their diagnosis. The healing power of sound may not have "tangible" proof of its benefits at times, but it is undeniable that it has an effect when you witness people's lives change right before your eyes.

As Eastern and Western healing philosophies come together in the present, we are finding that their practices seem to be very complimentary. We are able to see science and spirit (feeling) going hand in hand. I always recommend that my clients follow any protocols their doctor suggests while we work together. I also recommend they start paying attention to how they are feeling more often and where they are feeling it in their body. Our bodies are giving us messages all the time. Most of us are ignoring those messages or we are not aware of how to change. For example, the majority of people on the planet are in a constant state of "fight or flight" because of the stress we are experiencing in all facets of our life. It is not "bad" to be in "fight or flight" mode, it can save our lives. However, most people don't make time to (or know how to) rest and reset their system after the stressful or traumatic event occurs. When we don't make time to reset, we begin to experience dis-ease and pain within the body. Working with sound and intention to move out of this pattern is easy (with practice) and is possible for everyone to learn.

As I move through my own process of self-discovery, I am reminded that my voice is my most powerful healing instrument. I remember that the sound of our voices is created from the vibration of the vocal cords in our throat. When artists sing a song it's not just the vibration of the voice, it usually has a message behind it that has a vibration (feeling or intention) as well. The messages we share with others and ourselves have the potential to influence us into a space of allowing or resistance. In the process of finding our voice, through the awareness of our intentions behind it, what if we worked with sounds and loving intentions to hear the messages of our bodies clearly? What if we worked with the sound of our voice and directed it with the mind to different areas of the physical body to connect with that part of us in a different way? Dr. Mitchell Gaynor had clients experiencing cancer create their own personal life song to sing to themselves as they were going through treatment. They worked with old Sanskrit Bija Mantra sounds to envision their cells, in the mind, in harmony. Sounds with loving intention being directed throughout the body to heal… What a concept!

EXERCISE: BIJA MANTRA AND TONING

I encourage you to work with the sounds listed below to see how they feel within your body. In Vedic tradition, "Bija Mantras" are tools for the expansion of the mind by working with the power of sound and vibration. The literal translation of the word "Mantra" means "to liberate the mind". In Sanskrit a "seed" is called "Bija." As we work with the sound of our own voice to speak to parts of our body with these healing intentions, it is possible to be more aware of how we're feeling (vibrationally) inside. Just like when an instrument is out of tune, we make adjustments until the sound and instrument (the body) are in-tune. As you practice, maybe this becomes a part of your morning or evening ritual?

I also suggest that you do your own research on bija mantras and the chakras or energy centers of the body. Most of my learning on this journey has been my own curiosity and finding things on the internet that resonated and books recommended by friends, family and teachers. We have a world of information at our fingertips. Dive in and find what is there for You.

I suggest singing the sounds below with your eyes closed first and see where the mind leads you. Then, consciously direct the mind to bring the sound to a specific part of the body. Each of the sounds below is connected to a different chakra according to Vedic Healing. I encourage you to practice following where your mind takes you and directing your mind to the corresponding area of the body. Be aware of how you feel while practicing. Maybe even journal about it to gain more insights from yourself?

Each corresponding sound rhymes with "mom" and is listed with its chakra.

1. LAM (Root)
2. VAM (Sacral)
3. RAM (Solar Plex)
4. YAM (Heart)
5. HAM (Throat)
6. OM (Third Eye)
7. AUM (Crown)

Quote

"Our roots provide foundation and direction. They anchor us and align us in our purpose. They allow us to soar into our highest potentials. Always come back to the roots."

~ Jessica Neideffer

TOOL #14:
BEING GROUNDED WHEN CREATING

As we become more aware of our thoughts, or a master of being conscious, the more beneficial it is that we are grounded during our creation process. As our awareness grows, we are able to begin to transform our physical environment and experiences because we are able to shift out of unloving thoughts more quickly. And when we are in a loving space mentally, we are able to shift out of the "negative" vibration we may be emitting now that we're choosing to be more aware. Seeing and feeling yourself grounded is a practice. We can choose what grounded looks like in our mind. Again, I will remind you that there is no "right" or "wrong" in this process. Maybe you're a tree and you see roots connecting you deeply into the core of the earth. Now, imagine it in your mind and then actually feel those roots at the bottom of your feet. Challenge yourself to feel what the roots feel like coming out of the bottom of your feet. Are they thick and gnarly or are they thin and straggly? Connect deep into the core of the Earth. Maybe even see the core close to the surface as you connect so it doesn't seem so far out of reach. Remember, the brain does not know the difference between what we are experiencing in the mind with the eyes closed and what we experience with them open. If we have a bad dream, or we get pulled back into an uncomfortable memory, our bodies re-live it as the mind goes into it.

I'd also like to provide a different perspective of grounding for those who think that being grounded means they are stuck in one place. I see being grounded as having a healthy foundation to work from in the mind. I see being grounded as having a life-line to this space and time as we venture out into our thoughts and other aspects of the Self. I sometimes get the picture in my head of a deep diver out in the ocean. The diver has a certain amount of air in the tank and a destination to reach in a body of water that seems infinite. When a diver is going deep, they have a line connected to them so they are able to find their way back to the boat before running out of oxygen. I am reminded with this visual that I am an energetic being, and that I have a soul body (my oxygen), and I remember that I choose to be here first (my life-line). Being connected or grounded allows me to experience the soul energy of me without denying the choice to be in the physical realm.

When we are in a grounded state of being, the imagination is also able to expand "out of the box" of the limited mind because we've given it stability with this foundation. As we begin to visualize what we are creating, we see that we are building from this healthy foundation as well. If we start to see our vision going into a space that doesn't feel good in the body, we are able to go back to being grounded and bring in a new visual or old memory that is more pleasant. Meaning, if you wish to be more joyful, remember a time when you felt the most joy and bring yourself back to that moment in your life. Feel the energy of that moment in your body and then drop your physical body here and now into that vision. When you bring your present, physical body into the picture in the mind, you are integrating all aspects and versions of you at once. You show the mind that none are separate (past, present, future) and allow it to be more in alignment with the loving feeling we are choosing to move into. I see this as an easy way for us to practice this new pattern of loving thoughts more often.

Dropping your present self into the feeling of the vision brings the joy of that particular moment into this current space and time. By practicing being grounded and moving into a new possibility in the mind, it becomes possible to re-wire the brain and create a new neuropathway or pattern to follow. All we are doing is giving the mind a new thought or visual to go to instead of the old thoughts that may no longer serve. We are training the mind to go into a joyful space, instead of whatever unloving thoughts may have been attached to past experiences. The more joy-filled we are with our new thought patterns, the more unlimited we become in the manifestation process. I encourage you to be as creative and adventurous as possible with the things you wish to experience here on Earth. It is also helpful to be open to them when they arrive in a package that you didn't expect.

EXERCISE: GROUND | VISUALIZE | DROP IN

Choose the picture of "grounded" that works for you. Give the mind a focal point to come back to if it wanders. Practice being grounded while visualizing or imagining this picture and feeling it in the physical body. Once you have successfully connected with this feeling, bring the most joy-filled moment in your life into the mind. Allow yourself to feel this moment all over again in the brain with the eyes closed. Allow yourself to re-live the experience to the point where you are able to feel a physical sensation from the memory. Meaning, your chest or other part of your body has a warm, maybe even euphoric, tingly feeling. Maybe you feel a breeze move through you? As this feeling becomes visceral, imagine your present physical body dropping into the past joy-filled memory, connecting your past, present and future at once.

Allow yourself to be present with the feelings in your physical body. Spend some time simply experiencing this aspect of You in the moment. These experiences allow us to know ourselves more deeply by how we feel into them.

Quote

"Money is not the most important thing in the world. Love is. Fortunately, I love money."

~ Jackie Mason

TOOL #15:
CULTIVATING RELATIONSHIPS AND ABUNDANCE

We experience many relationships in the short life we live here on Earth including the one we have with money. Some people believe it is "the root of all evil" and others pray to it like it is a God. What most of us don't consider is that we have a relationship with this medium of exchange we call money. These pieces of paper and coins seem to make people do things that they might never think of until offered this "reward". I see most humans practicing this reward system every day as they commute at least an hour each way to work, to make money, to pay the bills, to do it all over again the next day. I see people working so many hours that they miss out on valuable time enjoying their loved ones and being in their passion. I recognize in my own work experiences to this point that I enjoyed them for the most part and am also able to see that with each job the main goal was to make more money. In our society, most see money as this thing that makes us important and the more of "it" we have the more important we feel. The real question is, "Why?".

As we grow from children into adults, we are taught that we must get a "good education" and "work hard" to get a "better job" so that we can seemingly be deemed worthy of the life we live. I'd like to remind humans that the people who made these "rules" did not have our best interests in mind. I see the purpose of this model as a way of keeping us in a cycle of unworthiness and shame because most people never achieve "enough" to deem themselves "successful". I like to remember that there is no "right" or "wrong" in the way we attract abundance or how much of it we have in our accounts. I like to remember that money is simply the exchange we work with to create here in this physical world. I also like to remember that when we attract anything into our lives there is always an intention behind it. I believe that our intention in anything we create has an effect on the outcome of the experience that we choose. However, most people are unaware of their intentions when asking money to be in a relationship with them.

In my own experience, I realize that there has been a pattern of lack and need in my relationship with money in the past. I would go to work because there was a "lack" of funds in my account and I "needed" to pay my bills. This has been a belief that I have carried with me since my first job at Denny's in the nineties. I remember taking the job because I dreamed of all those cash tips in my hand at the end of the day and it made me feel powerful. Fortunately, I enjoyed waiting tables and found that I was really good at it too. And, in the end, I was going to work just to pay the bills and get out at the end of the day to "check-out" and party. After five years working as a server, I was offered a chance to work in the high-tech world, saw more dollar signs and moved into it with the intention of acquiring more money. The first administrative job I had was at Hewlett-Packard in 1996 and I thought I had "arrived". I thought I was a "bad ass" because of all the money I was making, but I never asked myself why I felt this way.

The Little Book of Tools

As I continued to work in high-tech for the next twenty years, I looked for new jobs with the intention of making more money, so I could do and have more things. Again, I never really paid attention to the reasons behind making more money. The jobs I had paid enough, but I still had credit card debt from all the things I had to have and the things I wanted to do. I was not very aware, responsible or caring in my relationship with money. I would spend more than I would make every month and I imagine I have paid at least $100,000 in debt over the last 25 years. I occasionally experience this pattern of lack and need at times, but now I see it as an opportunity for me to look deeper within to see why the belief still exists.

What is also different now is the awareness of why I wish to attract money now. As my awareness changes, I give myself a choice in how I attract abundance in the first place. I see money as a partner in freedom and a means to share with others. When I pay my bills, I write hearts on the checks and feel gratitude for the abundance to pay them. When I am able to enjoy a vacation or buy something I've always wanted, I feel supported and loved in taking care of myself. I choose gratitude because it is the easiest state of being I am able to get into quickly. I am always able to find something to be grateful for in any situation. When I am being grateful my life runs smoothly and I experience less conflict.

How do you feel about money? What are you able to see about your relationship with money after reading the above? Maybe do the exercise below for a different perspective?

I encourage you to do this next exercise below without reading further or looking at the answers in the back of the book.

EXERCISE: THE MONEY EXERCISE

Answer the questions below with a simple "yes" or "no" as if Money is asking you.

Am I security for You?
Do you expect me to take care of you?
Do you expect me to make you happy?
Are you afraid of me?
Are you proud of our relationship?
Do you love me?
Do you tell the truth about our relationship?

Continued on next page...

Money Exercise Continued...

Now, take your answers and apply them to your relationship with an intimate partner. Imagine the intimate partner asking you the questions and these are the exact answers you give the person. Notice what comes up in your body when you imagine your response to an intimate partner instead of money. Did you answer "no" to loving money, which gave you an answer of "No, I don't love you" to your partner? There is no difference between your relationship with money or an intimate partner. Both are Relationships and Everything is Energy! If you answered all the questions "correctly", I'd like for you to consider "why" you answered them in this way and see what comes up.

If you felt the "need" to answer more than "yes" or "no" to any of the questions, I ask you to consider why as well. I have noticed when people are not being honest with themselves there are more words to the story they tell. I notice that the justification of their actions or feelings becomes more pronounced. When clients I work with begin to ramble about something, I ask them a simple yes or no question until they are honest with themselves. Sometimes, they refuse to answer yes or no because they do not want to give a definitive answer in that moment. I see this as not taking ownership for their feelings or actions. I also see this as limiting us in the manifestation of our desires. When we are not willing to take ownership, we are not being clear in our intentions and I have found that we are not able to create what we wish for because of this lack of clarity. Whether it be financial abundance or an intimate relationship, we will continue to attract it according to the beliefs or feelings we carry in the unconscious and conscious mind. The key to shifting out of any limiting patterns is to become aware of any unloving beliefs in the first place. And we do this by practicing the tools and exercises in this book. It is beneficial to practice on our own and to work with a healer to accelerate the process.

Quote

"The fastest way to manifest your heart's desires is to experience them, dream them, over and over in the mind. Live the vision in your mind to the point that you are able to feel it in your body with such impeccability that it has no choice but to manifest."

~ Jessica Neideffer

TOOL #16:
MANIFEST YOUR DREAMS & DESIRES

I feel like it's safe to say that everyone has experienced wanting something in life so "badly" that they had a hard time placing their attention on anything else, right? When we place our attention on someone or something, as energetic beings, we are able to send a pretty intense signal out with that desire. If it's a person, the recipient will usually pick up on the vibration we're putting out there. When it matches or resonates, people come together even when those vibrations are opposites, they are able to come together because everything is energy. It's like the old saying, "opposites attract". Sometimes, this works very well in a relationship and if there are not enough mutual things in common the individuals may be challenged to stay together over time. When we are working on consciously manifesting partners or things into our life, like a new home or job, we have to work within the realms of the imagination to begin creating here on earth. In my own process of creating, I have found that the fastest way to manifest into the now is to write my thoughts down with every detail I am able to fathom. Allowing myself to experience it all before it arrives. This way, when it does come to fruition, I recognize it by the way it feels, not necessarily how it looks.

As we begin to create consciously, we are made aware during this manifestation process there is a clearing that must happen as we move forward in our desire. Hence the previous pages of this book. All the tools I've shared are the clearing work that allows us to manifest clearly from the heart. When a person begins to imagine their dream, they are focused on it and at the same time, there is an unconscious dialogue running in the back of the mind. The unconscious dialogue or the "screaming voices" might not be in alignment with what is truly desired in the heart. Meaning, those voices might be saying "you're not good enough" or "you're never going to accomplish that" and what ends up being manifested are only parts of the dream. I see it as our channel being clogged by limiting beliefs and that the true desire is not able to come to form through us. I see it as sending mixed signals out into the atmosphere and receiving the same in return. Sometimes, this experience feels frustrating. I see this feeling of frustration as the wake-up call reminding me to check in with "why" I want something and if it is in alignment with my truth. What is my truth? My truth is that I am a BEing of Love and Light, We All Are. If what I am creating doesn't feel loving, I might want to look a little deeper.

When we start to peel back the layers and be aware of the beliefs that we have chosen, we will begin to see who we truly are through this process of self-discovery. At first, it may seem scary to see the unloving thoughts we have carried for so long, but as we open our eyes more, we see it is simply something we were told and not necessarily our truth. As we choose to be vulnerable and practice being safe in our own mind as we venture inward, we open the doors to limitless possibilities and allow our desires to be fulfilled. We also remember that faith and trust in our abilities is what allows us to create completely. The clearing work is what allows us to start manifesting from a more consistent place of love, which allows the things we ask for to arrive in the physical completely. All human beings desire to be loved, approved of, and accepted. As we choose to look at ourselves more deeply as we create, we allow ourselves to stop looking to others for validation of what it is we are creating. And by focusing our attention and intention inward, we step more into our power.

A really cool example for myself of my channel being more clear was when I realized it was time for me to move into my own office. Actually, I heard my higher self tell me it was time. I started looking on Craigslist and driving around downtown San Jose looking for available spaces. I made a list of all the qualities of my office. I wrote down all the details I could imagine, including the color and art on the walls. I imagined the space being within a 5-mile radius of my home. I wrote down the amount of rent I wanted to pay and what the chairs looked like in the place. I even imagined what it felt like sitting on those teal, velvet chairs in my mind before they even arrived. I looked for a couple of months until one day, I realized that every office I looked at was lacking free onsite parking. Once I added this desire to my list, my office appeared within a couple of days! The space was only three blocks from my home with free onsite parking and lovely neighbors. I was so shocked at how quickly it happened, it still took me two weeks to sign the rental agreement.

When we are manifesting a new partner or relationship, we must remember to be specific in the details as well. Even if we're not looking to be in a relationship with someone or we have a partner already, I encourage people to create a partner quality list in order to see what they desire from their heart for humans as a whole. Really, what we are doing by creating this list is seeing what we love the most about ourselves and what we desire to share with the world. This list is our own unique expression of what it is to be human from our perspective while remembering that ALL others are correct as well. When we write out these desires and love of who we are, we are again validating our experience, and this is truly loving ourselves. The list is not just for intimate partners. A list can be created for business partners and friendships too. Maybe you are looking to surround yourself with new friends? Maybe you wish to be part of a new community? I suggest creating this list of all the qualities you desire in order to manifest clearly.

When we make time to sit quietly with our Self and write down or draw our dreams, we are loving ourselves. When we write down these desires on a piece of paper, with a pen, with our hand, we are bringing them into the physical world. Now, there is a piece of paper to look at if we get off track. Now, there is something to remind us of the plans we are manifesting. Since we are changing constantly, I find it helpful to have something in writing to hold us accountable as well. I see it like a contract with our Self. We have the ability to change the contract at any time and it is there to keep us on the path to creating our dreams.

EXERCISE: PARTNER QUALITY LIST

To practice manifesting into the physical you could start with something big or small. It can be anything, really. I highly recommend creating a Partner Quality List with the most loving intentions to begin. I suggest sitting quietly and coming from the heart with loving thoughts about this person. Whether you have a partner already does not matter. The purpose of the exercise is to bring our desires into the physical by putting them in writing. Your current partner may already embody many of the things you desire. And, if they don't seem to, it may help to open the lines of communication regarding what you wish to experience with them. Maybe it is a way for you to see a new way of BEing with your Self and this person.

Create your list with only positive desires like: loves themselves unconditionally, loves to cook, is compassionate, enjoys hiking and being outdoors, etc. Remember, most of what you write will be things that you love about yourself or that you wish to experience with others. When you're finished, maybe draw some hearts on it and place it in a gift box and place that box in a safe space. For example, my list has hearts drawn all over it with a little drop of rose oil on the paper. I keep it folded neatly in an old coin purse that belonged to my Grandma Betty with her rosary beads in it. I keep the coin purse in my night stand drawer, so I am able to view it every once in a while.

Remember, this list can be updated any time and there is no need to dwell on it or obsess if it doesn't happen as quickly as the mind thinks it should. Maybe check in with it when you feel something shift or change within you as the energy that you created it with will change as you choose to be more present and aware with your Self and your thoughts.

THE BEGINNING

There is a thing we call an "ending" here in this human life, but I prefer to see it as a "beginning" because we are forever evolving like the Universe. It continues growing and expanding and remnants of what was and what will be, remain present in some subtle way. ALL continues to exist simultaneously like the visions in our mind, some seen, some unseen. Human beings are made of the same materials as the stars and the planets. And, if the Universe is "endless", I imagine us humans to be the same. I see us limitless and expansive, capable of creating our heart's desires as we become more aware of ourselves and how we choose to create in this world. I believe we come into this world with the purpose of expressing love in our own unique way. The opinions of others and the beliefs we choose to carry are the things that keep us limited in this self-expression and the physical body that we experience life in, one of the things that makes us seem separate.

I invite you to imagine what our experience will be like when we are able to let go of the labels, limiting beliefs, and insecurities that we hold simply out of fear of the unknown. I assure you, the unknown only feels "scary" sometimes because we forget that the feeling of excitement comes from the same energetic space within. What if we simply replaced "I am scared" with "I am excited"? I am not saying to ignore our gut instincts when they're telling us to run. I am saying that when we feel those butterflies in our stomach and we feel a little uncomfortable, we just might be on the "right" track. What if we stopped being afraid of our own success? What would we be able to create with this freedom from fear? Remembering that as we allow ourselves to be successful and confident that we project these loving energies out giving others permission to do and be the same. What if we chose to support others in their endeavors emotionally and contributed to their vision of success financially? I see these ideas as possibilities of the success of Every One.

I imagine the tools and exercises in this book will support everyone in becoming more aware of the Self in order to give us more choices in our experiences. I imagine us all being able to observe more and react less in our interactions with Self and others. I imagine us ALL choosing collaboration over competition and remembering what compassion and community are again. The intention of writing this book was to provide a simple tool box that includes practical, easy ways of shifting our perspective in order to change our experience. I work with these tools every day and find them to be quite powerful when I practice them impeccably. When I'm not practicing, I notice that my day tends to be a bit more challenging. I imagine if you've read the book this far, that it resonates. If you find it doesn't, please share it with someone else who you feel it might.

I encourage you to work with this book as a guide and see it as a compilation of suggestions and ideas, none of which must be believed or utilized. Simply consider it one of the many "Bibles" out there today. And when I suggest the term "Bible" I mean it as an acronym. For me it stands for: Basic Instructions Before Leaving Earth. I realize there are many to choose from and I encourage you to continue seeking the guides that resonate with you. I also remind you that it isn't "wrong" if it doesn't resonate, it is simply meant for someone else. Check in with your heart and ask how it is feeling in each moment. Be present with how your body is feeling because it will give you the clues to the answers you seek. And always feel your feet firmly planted on the Earth. When we work from a healthy and stable foundation, no person, place or thing is able to move us from our path or purpose. Thank You for making the time to consider different perspectives as you work with this book. I am honored that you made the time to read it.

I wish us all the best in our new beginnings here and beyond!

ANSWERS TO THE MONEY EXERCISE IN TOOL #15

Am I security for You?   No

When we put the responsibility of our security on someone, we are expecting them to make us feel secure, when really, we choose to feel secure, or not.

Do you expect me to take care of you?   No

We are putting an expectation on another to care for us and we are not being responsible for our Self.

Do you expect me to make you happy?   No

We are not taking ownership of our own joy and happiness.

Are you afraid of me? No   No

Are you proud of our relationship?   Yes

Do you love me?   Yes

Do you tell the truth about our relationship? Yes

REFERENCES

Chavez, Caesar. "Our language is the reflection of ourselves". *Brainy Quote.* URL: https://www.brainyquote.com/quotes/ cesar_chavez_389927

Hay, Louise. *You Can Heal Your Life.* Carlsbad: Hay House.1984. Print.

Ruiz, Miguel Angel. *The Four Agreements.* San Rafael: Amber Allen.1997. Print.

Randolph, John Price. *The Abundance Book.* Carlsbad: Hay House. 1987. Print.

Abraham-Hicks. Worthiness quote. Facebook, 13/03/13, URL: https://www.facebook.com/Abraham.Hicks/posts/worthiness-in-very-simple-terms-means-i-have-found-a-way-to-let-the-energy-reach/308432325950096/.

Dooley, Mike. Choose them wisely: Thoughts become things! New York: Atria Books. 2009. Print.

Castaneda, Carlos. *The Wheel of Time.* Washington Square Press: New York.1998. Print.

Marshall, Kerry James. "At a certain point". *Brainy Quote.* URL: https://www.brainyquote.com/authors/kerry_james_marshall

Warhol, Andy. "My fascination with letting images repeat". *Brainy Quote*. URL: https://www.brainyquote.com/quotes/andy_warhol_597871

Tolle, Eckhart. *The Power of Now*. Vancouver: Namaste Publishing. 1999. Print.

Frank, Anne. The Diary of Anne Frank. Doubleday: New York. 1967. Print.

Szasz, Thomas. "Every act of conscious learning". *Brainy Quote*. URL: https://www.brainyquote.com/authors/thomas_szasz

Mason, Jackie. "Money is not the most important thing". Brainy Quote. URL: https://www.azquotes.com/quote/527441

Brodie, Renee. *The Healing Tones of Crystal Bowls*. Aroma Art Ltd. 1996. Print.

Gaynor, Mitchell. *The Healing Power of Sound*. Boston: Shambhala. 2002. Print.

Van der kolk, Bessel. *The Body Keeps the Score: Brain, Mind and Body in the Healing of Trauma*. New York: Penguin Books. 2014. Print.

Swan, Teal. "The Connection Process". Youtube. 13/05/16. URL: https://www.youtube.com/watch?v=8eHVH3iuRig&t=56s

CPSIA information can be obtained
at www.ICGtesting.com
Printed in the USA
LVHW050612040619
620063LV00002B/231